A Point in History

John G. Morgan

A Point in History

The Battle of Point Pleasant

John G. Morgan

WEST VIRGINIA

Library of Congress Card Catalog Number: 2001095079
ISBN: 0-9667246-6-6

First Edition, First Printing

Printed in the United States of America

Book and Cover Design: Mark S. Phillips/Marketing+Design Group

Project Coordinator: Eddie E. Lowe/Main Street Point Pleasant

Chapters 1-19 inclusive were originally published as a series of newspaper articles just after the bicentennial celebration of the Battle of Point Pleasant (1975).
Reprinted courtesy of the *Charleston Gazette*.

Additional information copiled for the appendices came from the following sources:
Appendices I, II, III: Col. Charles Lewis Chapter, DAR
Appendix IV: Fort Randolph Committee
Appendix V: Diana Johnson, Battle Days Committee

Find out more about Point Pleasant at:
www.pointpleasantwv.org

Main Street Point Pleasant
305 Main Street
Point Pleasant, WV 25550

DiscoveryPress
WEST VIRGINIA
945 Fourth Avenue, Suite 200A
Huntington, WV 25701

Table of Contents

PREFACE

The first nineteen chapters in this book were originally published in 1975 by the *Charleston Gazette*, Charleston, West Virginia.

The Point Pleasant Restoration Foundation wishes to thank the *Gazette* for its contribution in the reprinting of this publication.

By publishing this information, we preserve this work for students of history to study and draw their independent conclusions regarding the events surrounding the Battle of Point Pleasant.

Whatever is decided, we believe it is important to preserve this information for posterity.

Eddie E. Lowe
Main Street Point Pleasant
Point Pleasant, West Virginia

Dedication

Publication was made possible
by the generosity of the
Gordon C. and Mildred R. Jackson Foundation.

Lord Dunmore Heads for Frontier

Williamsburg, Va., July 10, 1774

Lord Dunmore left the Governor's Palace today for a trip to the western frontier.

His lordship, the Royal Governor of Virginia, said he wants to get a first hand view of frontier conditions along the Ohio River and talk peace with the Indians.

His departure came in the wake of frontier reports of new Indian uprisings. It gave a new twist to swirling events that have this colonial capital in turmoil.

DUNMORE, 42, is a short, thick, sturdy man with a hoary head. He has a reputation as a tactless, ambitious type, but he also is an affable fellow who communicates easily with common soldiers. He marches with them and carries his own knapsack.

A native of Scotland, he has this full name and title: John Murray, 4th Earl Of Dunmore, Viscount Fincastle, Baron of Blair, of Monlin and of Tillimet.

As governor of Virginia, he presides over a vast domain with an estimated population of about 500,000, including about 5,000 who live here. Before coming here less than three years ago, he served as governor of New York about a year.

Despite his background and titles, and his unquestioned loyalty to King George III, he delights in championing the cause of Virginia.

On this mission, he has the backing of the Virginia House of Burgesses, which authorized him to exercise his full powers against possible invasion of Indians.

The *Virginia Gazette* commented on the gravity of the situation:

"We believe with too much certainty that an Indian war is inevitable, as many outrages have lately happened on the frontiers; but whether the Indians or white people are most to blame, we cannot determine.

UNDER THE 1768 treaty of Fort Stanwix, the Ohio River is supposed to be the dividing line between Virginians and Indians. But residents on both sides have crossed the river in increasing numbers and engaged in plundering and killing.

The mass murder of close relatives and friends of Mingo Chief Logan ranks among the most brutal acts ever committed on the frontier. This is essentially what happened on the morning of last April 30:

Four Indians left their village near the mouth of Yellow Creek and crossed the Ohio River to Baker's Bottom, in the northern neck of Virginia, where they normally bought supplies.

There, at Joshua Baker's house, a party of whites supplied the Indians with liquor until they were drunk and tricked them into unloading their guns in games of marksmanship.

Then the whites murdered the four Indians and about six more who came to see what the shooting was about. Among the dead were a brother and sister of Logan.

The tragic news soon reached Logan, a fine specimen of a man, tall and straight as a spear shaft, peace-loving, greatly admired by many of the whites and known for his noble loyalty to his friends.

A scowl spread over his countenance when he learned the truth. He raised his tomahawk and swore personal vengeance against the whites.

THE PROSPECTS OF WAR are causing something close to panic

among some settlers near the frontier. Many are clustering in improvised blockhouses, and others are fleeing eastward to populated areas.

The worsening situation is complicated by a hot border dispute between Virginia and Pennsylvania in the Pittsburgh area at the forks of the Ohio.

"Land fever," meaning the urge of speculators and people in high places to acquire large tracts, may very well have a bearing on the boundary's dispute and the impending war with the Indians. His lordship himself has a bad case of land fever.

A new phenomenon on the tumultuous governmental scene at Williamsburg may have some relationship to the threat of war with the Indians. It is a rare manifestation of resistance to English rule. It popped up unexpectedly six weeks ago in the House of Burgesses.

Among House members present for the unusual chain of events were two brothers, who represent counties that sprawl westward from the Blue Ridge Mountains to the Ohio River.

They are Col. Andrew Lewis, 53, of Botetourt County in the southwestern part of the state, and Col. Charles Lewis, 38, of Augusta County in the northwestern part. Each also serves as the county lieutenant or top officer for the militia in his county.

AMONG OTHERS PRESENT were Col. George Washington, 42, of Fairfax County, under whom the Lewis brothers served in the French and Indian War; Thomas Jefferson, 31, of Albemarle County; and Patrick Henry, 38, of Hanover County.

Jefferson and Henry were among leaders who successfully pushed for adoption of a resolution that set aside June 1 as a "day of fasting, humiliation and prayer" on behalf of the people of Boston.

The May 24 resolution was in direct reaction to passage of the Boston Port Bill by the British Parliament. The bill, effective June 1, closed Boston Harbor until the tea destroyed by the Boston Tea Party last Dec. 16 can be paid for. On May 26,

Dunmore did his duty as a loyal officer of the King. He dissolved the legislative assembly.

Not to be outdone, 89 members of the dissolved House retired to the Apollo Room of Raleigh's Tavern, formed an association and agreed that a general congress should be held annually. The first meeting is scheduled for Sept. 5 in Philadelphia.

REGARDLESS of the upheaval, certain legislators and Lord Dunmore remain close friends. Washington spent the evening with him on May 25. On the next day, the very day the House was dissolved, Washington rode with his lordship to the Dunmore farm and had breakfast there.

During the evening of May 27, Washington and many other legislators attended a ball in honor of Lady Dunmore.

In terms of land interests, Washington, Lord Dunmore and Col. Andrew Lewis have much in common. Vast tracts of land, granted by Dunmore in the name of the king, are held by Washington, Lewis and others on the Great Kanawha and Ohio Rivers.

This land is included in a proposed 14th colony called Vandalia. The new colonial capital is to be on a point of land at the confluence of the two rivers.

His lordship, during his term as governor of New York, entertained visions of great landed estates. He circumvented the king's limitation of 1,000 acres per individual and obtained 51,000 acres for himself in Lake Champlain country. This was done with the cooperation of 51 friends.

DURING HIS TERM as governor here, he petitioned the king for a grant of 100,000 acres in Augusta County. The petition was denied with a note that the land would be divided and sold to the highest bidder.

As his lordship begins his westward trip today, county officers are responding to his earlier orders to call out the militia and organize for war.

The orders, given in his capacity as commander-in-chief of the colonial militia, require the Lewis brothers and other county officers to prepare the troops to follow the enemy into his own country.

"I shall, at my own risk, endeavor to furnish you with powder and ball," Lord Dunmore told the officers in a circular letter.

Two scouts were sent along the frontier to warn survey teams of approaching danger. One is Michael Stoner, and the other is a lean, strong, 38-year-old man named Daniel Boone.

Governor's Palace, Williamsburg, Va.

CHAPTER

Delaware Chief, Dunmore Meet

PITTSBURGH, Va., Sept. 10, 1774

"I tell you that I am extremely rejoiced at your arrival here, as you are our esteemed elder brother."

So spoke Delaware Chief White Eyes to Lord Dunmore at a peace conference here.

"I acknowledge myself your elder brother, and shall upon every occasion manifest my regard toward you," answered his lordship.

Dunmore, the royal governor of Virginia, went into conference with the friendly Delaware chief and other Indian leaders after arriving here from Williamsburg a few days ago.

Not present for the conference was Chief Cornstalk of the Shawnees, rated as the most murderous and menacing of all the tribes in the limitless wilderness west of the Ohio River.

Mohawk Chief Big Apple Tree tried to speak on behalf of Cornstalk and his tribe.

White Eyes volunteered to arrange for a meeting between Shawnee leaders and Dunmore and his officers. His lordship declared:

"I will be ready and willing to hear any good speeches which the Shawnees may have to deliver to me, either at Wheeling, where I soon propose to be or, if they should not meet me there, at the Little Kanawha, or somewhere lower down the river."

There were many long speeches and exchanges of gifts during the conference. White Eyes offered a string with these words:

"I wipe the sweat and dust from your eyes by this string, and remove the fatigue that you have had during your journey; and also I clear and open your ears that you may readily comprehend and hear what our brothers have to say to you."

LORD DUNMORE declared as he gave a condolence present:

"With these trifling goods I cover the grave of your deceased friends, that the remembrance of your grief upon that occasion may be buried in total oblivion."

By simply talking with the Indians, his lordship achieved a major goal during his current visit to this trouble spot on the Western frontier.

Although the results were disappointing, the conference at least strengthened ties with his Indian friends, and there is further promise of downriver peace talks with the Shawnees in the near future.

Dunmore left the Governor's Palace at Williamsburg two months ago today to make the long trek across the Blue Ridge and Allegheny Mountains to the frontier along the Ohio River. On the way he made a big decision.

At Greenway Court, the spacious estate of Lord Fairfax near Winchester, he made the decision to recruit and personally lead a large striking force against the Indians in the Ohio wilderness.

HE UNFOLDED a plan for structuring the northern division of the Army under his personal direction, in addition to the southern division being organized by Col. Andrew Lewis at the Great Levels on the Greenbrier River.

The idea of the large striking force was born with the failure of a small one.

A force of about 400 men, commanded by Maj. Angus McDonald, moved up the Muskingum River in the Ohio woodlands Aug. 2.

The objective was the Indian village of Wapatomica. But by the time the men arrived there, after engaging in minor skirmishing, the village was deserted. McDonald gave this terse report:

"I and my party attacked the upper Shawnee towns. I destroyed their cornfields, burnt their cabins, and took three scalps and one prisoner. I had two men killed and six wounded.'

By any standard it was an ineffective strike. The Indians, instead of being scared into staying in their villages, marauded on the frontier with renewed vigor.

When the 400 men returned, Lord Dunmore incorporated them in a northern division of approximately 1,000 men. The 600 additional men were drawn largely from Frederick and Berkeley Counties.

A FREDERICK County regiment of 500 men was formed under Col. William Crawford. A Berkeley regiment of equal size was organized with Col. Adam Stephen as the commander.

From Greenway Court, his lordship wrote to Lord Dartmouth, the English secretary of state for the American colonies, told him of plans to hit some Indian villages on the Scioto River in the Ohio wilderness, and added:

"If I can possibly fall upon those lower towns undiscovered, I think I shall be able to put an end to this most cruel war in which there is neither honor, pleasure nor profit."

Incidentally, during the early months and into the summer of this year, the land-loving Dunmore received six grants totaling 3,465 acres in Hampshire County from Lord Fairfax. One was a 400-acre tract surveyed by George Washington.

The twin regiments moved out of Greenway Court in late August and marched down Braddock's Road. They arrived at the South Branch of the Potomac Aug. 30, and continued by way of Fort Cumberland to the mouth of Redstone Creek on the Monongahela River, where the two regiments separated.

At the separation point, the Berkeley men under Stephen pushed across country with a herd of beef cattle toward Wheeling. The Frederick men, marching with Lord Dunmore and Crawford, proceeded to Pittsburgh.

The Frederick regiment of 500 men was joined here by 200 men from the new district of West Augusta under the command of Maj. John Connolly.

Connolly, who serves as Lord Dunmore's agent on civil and military affairs in this area, is a swashbuckling, controversial character on the frontier.

Some traders in the area think Connolly is promoting war by his aggressive behavior toward Indians and Pennsylvanians. An open letter, issued by him last April was widely viewed as a declaration of war against Indians.

His conduct once landed him in a Pennsylvania jail. But he talked his way out, gathered some militiamen, stormed the jail, and sent three justices of the peace to prison in Staunton, VA.

There is evidence that Connolly and Lord Dunmore have a cozy business and military relationship.

During their association of approximately one year, the name of the key military establishment here has been changed from Fort Pitt to Fort Dunmore.

AND CONNOLLY has received a 2,000-acre land grant at the falls of the Ohio, deep in a southwestern area that the Shawnees call "Can-tuc-kee" (sacred hunting ground).

Connolly and a partner plan to build a town at the falls. They have advertised lots for sale.

Pittsburgh is fast becoming a substantial town here at the forks of the Ohio. There are several hundred cabins near Fort Dunmore, which is regarded today as the most important fort on the western frontier as far as Virginians are concerned.

There are many boundary line questions. The overriding question today is: Pittsburgh, Virginia, or Pittsburgh, Pennsylvania? Virginia claims the town today.

A 21-year-old surveyor is among Lord Dunmore's men. He is a heavily built man with unquailing blue eyes and shaggy brows. His name is George Rogers Clark.

CHAPTER

Camp Noise Shatters the Quiet

CAMP UNION, Va., Sept. 12, 1774

This is a noisy, busy place. Hundreds of frontiersmen are arriving and leaving for a long march over the mountains and down the Great Kanawha River to fight the Indians.

Men are shouting commands and marching around to the tune of fife and drums. Cattle and horses are milling around, mooing and neighing in a most unusual fashion.

This is Camp Union, so named because it is the gathering place for the southern division of Lord Dunmore's army.

DESPITE ALL the noise, there are regulations. Woods are to be scoured two miles around for any signs of Indians, no ammunition is to be wasted, and liquors aren't to be distributed in quantities that would make the troops drunk.

The setting here is a normally quiet place just west of the Greenbrier River and in a beautiful bluegrass region on a plateau called the "Great Levels." It is made all the more attractive by the presence of a spring that produces cool clear waters in large volume.

Excitement reached a new high Sept. 1 with the first appearance in camp of Col. Andrew Lewis, the division commander. A tall, imposing figure with a full, florid face and dark brown eyes, he strode around the grounds like a man born to command.

"He looks like a genius of the forest, and the very ground trembles under him as he walks along," an admirer once said of him. Lewis, 53, is a man of vast military experience. He fought side by side with Col. George Washington through most of the French and Indian War and was wounded at the Battle of Fort Necessity.

HIS BROTHER, Col. Charles Lewis, 38, who arrived here earlier to take charge of the Augusta regiment, is regarded as the idol of the army. He also served with Washington and is well known as a gallant Indian fighter and frontiersman.

The third-ranked officer on the scene here is the extraordinary Col. William Fleming, 45, a surgeon who received his medical education at the University of Edinburgh in Scotland. This man of culture, who enjoys unbounded popularity with the troops, has charge of the Botetourt regiment.

Col. William Preston, a central figure in the entire military operation against the Indians, hasn't reported to camp. Because of the serious illness of his wife, he will remain at his home in Smithfield for this campaign.

ANOTHER PEAK of excitement came on Sept. 6 when Col. Charles Lewis marched out of camp with about 600 men, 108 head of cattle and 500 packhorses carrying 54,000 pounds of flour, large quantities of salt and numerous kettles and tools.

The younger Lewis brother, with scouts and axe men moving ahead of him and his curious cavalcade, marched over a high hill and vanished into the wilderness.

His first order of business is to march to the mouth of Elk River and start building canoes for transportation of flour to the mouth of the Great Kanawha.

Soon after Lewis left, Col. William Christian arrived with a group of men from Fincastle County. Christian. 32, has served in the House of Burgesses with the Lewis Brothers.

Col. John Field, a daring, 54-year-old officer with an

independent company of 40 men from Culpepper County, left here Sept. 7, following the trail blazed by Col. Charles Lewis.

Still another peak in excitement is occurring today with the departure of Col. Andrew Lewis and Col. Fleming with 450 men, the remaining cattle and 200 packhorses loaded with flour.

By and large, the men coming and going here are a remarkable body of soldiers. Many are veterans of the French and Indian War. Nearly all have been engaged in some form of border warfare.

They are strong, determined, weather beaten men from stockaded hamlets, lonely clearings an all kinds of cabins and camps in the hills and hollows of vast timberlands in western Virginia.

THE MEN ARE to live largely on beef and bread in this campaign. Beef cattle were driven here from southern counties west of the Blue Ridge Mountains. Flour, ground by water mills in the Shenandoah Valley, was transported here by packhorses from Warm Springs.

Supplies of ammunition include lead from the mines at Fort Chiswell on upper New River and black powder manufactured near Natural Bridge.

Col. Andrew Lewis and other top officers decided on this rendezvous point in response to earlier communications from Lord Dunmore, now in the Pittsburgh area with the northern division of the army.

On June 10 of this year. Dunmore alerted key officers in this Virginia militia to hold their men in readiness for action against the Indians. In a follow-up letter July 12, Dunmore told Col. Andrew Lewis:

By no means wait any longer for them to attack you . . . raise all the men you think willing and able to go down immediately to the mouth of the Great Kanawha and there build a fort.

His lordship further suggested that, if Lewis could raise enough men, he should proceed across the Ohio River from the mouth of the Kanawha and destroy Indian villages.

Twelve days later, Dunmore suggested an alternate plan of action. He told Lewis:

"I desire you to raise a respectable body of men and join me either at the mouth of the Great Kanawha or Wheeling, as is most convenient for you."

A third message from Dunmore near the end of August directed that Lewis meet him at the mouth of the Little Kanawha River. Lewis didn't comply. He said it wasn't in his power to change the plans to go to the mouth of the Great Kanawha.

About 1,500 officers and men in the southern division were formally organized here in two regiments, one battalion and four independent companies, all under Col. Andrew Lewis, in this manner:

AUGUSTA COUNTY Regiment (600 men). Col. Charles Lewis commanding, with captains John Dickinson, George Moffatt, George Matthews, John Skidmore, John Lewis, William Nalle, Samuel McDowell, Alexander McClanahan, Andrew Lockridge, Samuel Wilson and Benjamin Harrison.

The Culpepper County Minute Men (40 men) with Col. John Field.

Botetourt County Regiment (450 men), Col. Fleming commanding, with captains Philip Love, John Lewis, John Stuart, James Ward, Matthew Arbuckle, John Murray, Robert McClanahan and Henry Pauling.

Plus the Bedford County Riflemen (44 men} with Capt. Thomas Buford.

Fincastle County Battalion (350 men). Col. Christian commanding, with captains William Russell, Joseph Crockett, William Campbell, Anthony Bledsoe, Evan Shelby, William Herbert and John Floyd.

Plus the Dunmore County Volunteers (40 men) with Capt. Thomas Slaughter: and the Kentucky Pioneers (27 men) with Capt. James Harrod.

Other key personnel include Maj. Thomas Posey, chief commissary officer; The Rev. Terry, chaplain; Capt. Matthew Arbuckle, chief guide; Frederick Burley, chief Indian spy; James Hughes, packhorse master; William McClure, chief cattle driver; John Warwick, chief butcher and John Coalter, carpenter.

Many members of the southern division are blood relatives or in-laws. Among them are Capt. John Lewis of Botetourt, son of Andrew; and Capt. John Lewis of Augusta, son of Thomas who is a brother of Andrew and Charles.

Capt. Evan Shelby is the father of Lt. Isaac Shelby and James Shelby, all in the same company. Capt. Alexander McClanahan and Capt. Robert McClanahan are brothers. Lt. John Sevier and Sgt. Valentine Sevier are brothers.

Col. William Fleming is married to Nancy Christian, a sister of Col. William Christian. Col. Christian and Capt. William Campbell are married to sisters of Patrick Henry, the Virginia legislator.

Mouth of Elk Bustling Place

MOUTH OF THE ELK, Va., Sept. 27, 1774

Sounds of axes and the general activity of men, horses and cattle break the stillness of a dense forest at the meeting place of two beautiful rivers here.

Men under the command of Col. Andrew Lewis in the southern division of Lord Dunmore's army are converting logs into dugout canoes. They are encamped on the east side of Elk River near the point that it feeds into the Great Kanawha.

Work is nearing completion on 27 canoes to be used in transporting flour and other supplies approximately 60 miles downstream to the confluence of the Great Kanawha and Ohio rivers.

At that point Lewis hopes to hear more from Lord Dunmore on plans for attacking Indian villages on the western side of the Ohio.

Col. Charles Lewis, brother of the division commander, arrived here Sept. 21 with approximately 600 men in the Augusta County regiment, along with a large herd of beef cattle and 400 pack horses carrying flour.

THE COMMANDER and the Botetourt County men arrived here Sept. 23, along with 200 horses laden with flour and a large number of additional cattle.

Independent companies from other areas have increased the ranks of both regiments. There are about 1,100 men here today.

Approximately 1,000 men, exclusive of officers, certain others on duty and the sick, answered a roll call today.

There are 32 on the sick list. In addition there are 23 captains, 25 lieutenants, 19 ensigns, 79 sergeants, three fifers and nine drummers. Among those who draw special duty are armorers, butchers and officer servants called batmen.

There are no white settlers within the area near the mouth of the Elk. The place looks as if it belongs to the Indians, wild animals, trees, rivers and the sky.

HOWEVER, 20 miles up the Kanawha, at the mouth of Kelly's Creek, lives the family of William Morris, Sr. He and members of his family comprise what is regarded as the first firmly established white settlement in the Kanawha Valley.

Six of the Morris sons reportedly joined Lewis' army when it marched by the Morris home earlier this month. They are William Morris, Jr., 28, and his five younger brothers, Henry, Leonard, Joshua, Levi and John.

The Morris cabins, built last summer, are near the mouth of Kelly's Creek. The stream was named for Walter Kelly, killed by Indians at his home near there last spring.

The two regiments, now encamped here, marched about 100 miles from Camp Union on the Great Levels near the Greenbrier River. They were led by Capt. Matthew Arbuckle, chief scout for the entire expedition.

Following old buffalo trails and carving new ones where necessary, the 1,100 men marched over rugged mountains and through deep and gloomy woods.

The Augusta regiment made the trip in 15 days. The Botetourt regiment, following approximately the same route and with less carving to do, arrived here in 11 days.

Marching with Col. Andrew Lewis was the Botetourt regimental commander, Col. William Fleming, a thoughtful, careful man with a medical education.

Fleming keeps a daily journal and orderly book on the travels and other activities of his regiment. He writes occasional letters to his wife and to key military personnel.

AT THE BEGINNING of each entry in his journal, he sketches the standard symbol for the sun, moon or planet with which the day of the week is identified. He also notes the password for the day.

For example, his regiment's march began at Camp Union on Sept. 12 under the sign of the moon, for which Monday was named. The password was "Frederick."

The first stop was called Camp Pleasant, on a branch of Muddy Creek. At this point a report was received that a man named Clay was killed by an Indian while deer hunting apart from the main body of troops attached to the Augusta regiment.

The Indian was shot by Clay's companion, named Coward, but another Indian got away and presumably spread the word that Lewis' army was coming. This incident has contributed to an eerie feeling among the troops that their movements are constantly being observed by Indians from every high hill or ridge.

Generally, after crossing Muddy Creek Mountain, the troops walked along Walkers Creek and Buffalo Lick Fork, tributaries of Meadow River. They moved through small forests of chestnut trees, crossed some steep little ridges and Great and Little Laurel Run, and went by a hunter's camp on Mann's Creek.

ON SEPTEMBER 19, one week after leaving Camp Union, the regiment crossed Gauley Mountain and camped at the head of Rich Creek. On that date there were frequent showers of rain between periods of sunshine.

On the next day Rich Creek was crossed several times, and Gauley River was forded at what Fleming described as an ugly stony place. The route avoided the great gorge worn by New River.

The regiment moved through Kelly's Creek bottoms, where there are abundant growths of papaw, beech and flowering poplar trees. Leatherwood bushes, pea vines and buffalo grass also grow there.

On Sept. 21 the line of march moved out of Kelly's Creek to the north bank of the Great Kanawha, which Fleming described as about 200 yards wide with high hills on each side. Farther downstream he was fascinated by the sight of gaseous, burning springs that would consume almost anything thrown into them.

"We endeavored to extinguish one of the springs by covering it with green grass, without effect as it consumed the grass," he said. The Botetourt troops camped beside the Kanawha near the springs. The password was "Charlestown." The next day they marched to the Elk and united with the Augusta regiment. Along the way they found an Indian track 14 inches long.

Today, after four days in camp, Fleming pondered the general situation and wrote a letter to his wife, Nancy. He told her that the southern division was within five days march of the Ohio River and that five scouts had been dispatched to the mouth of the Great Kanawha in search of Lord Dunmore.

IN FLIGHTS OF rhetoric and strong religious feeling, he added:

> "Remember, my dear girl, that the Divine Being is omnipresent as well as omnipotent, that He rides on the wings of the tempest, and directs the artillery of Heaven, beholds with serenity the rage of battle and directs each deadly shaft where to strike — for a sparrow falls not to the ground without His knowledge. . . .
>
> "Therefore, my dear, think of me as safe on the expedition, though we should have a skirmish or two with the Indians as if at home. And if it should be the will of God that I should fall, I must and cannot otherwise think, but that he who dies in the service of and defense of his country, dies in an act of religion, and circumstances considered, dies the death of the righteous, but my dear I hope in a few months to have the pleasure of personally telling you and my little son more particularly of our proceedings and till then I recommend you, him and the family to the protection of that Being who is equally present at this moment, and at all times with you and me."

CHAPTER

PEACEFUL CAMP—1,100 ARMED MEN

CAMP POINT PLEASANT, Va., Oct. 9,1774

Under giant trees in early autumnal glory and on pointed land between quietly flowing waters, about 1,100-armed Virginians are encamped here today, a peaceful Sunday.

On one side of the camp, the broad Ohio River has the appearance of a lake. On the other, the Great Kanawha River resembles a protective estuary.

Incidentally, Col. Andrew Lewis, commander of the troops here, is one of seven men who owns this point of ground as part of a 51,320-acre tract. The boundary line follows the east bank of the Ohio River upstream, goes around a big bend and cuts back across country to the Great Kanawha.

The tract was granted to the seven in 1772 by Lord Dunmore in recognition of prior military service and in the name of King George III. Under a similar grant made last year, Lewis is one of eight owners of 21,491 acres in the Pocatalico River area.

TO REACH THIS point of land between two rivers, the Virginians marched about 160 miles from Camp Union on the Great Levels near the Greenbrier River. All troops made the march in a month or less, with timeouts of seven to nine days for building canoes at the mouth of Elk River.

A flotilla of canoes, loaded with flour and other items, was launched into the Great Kanawha at the mouth of the Elk about the time the troops left there more than a week ago to begin the final march to the camp site here.

One canoe was upset, causing the loss of two guns and some baggage, and several bags of flour were set afloat. Canoe men recovered all bags, but two were extremely wet.

Col. William Fleming took note on the day of departure from the Elk that four men had deserted. He added that desertion "has been pretty frequent since we left the levels, and likewise the theft of flour and provisions."

Many packhorses, used in transporting flour over the mountains to the Elk, were returned to Camp Union. Some were retained to carry other burdens for the remainder of the journey.

On Sept. 30 the troops broke camp on the east side of Elk River, forded it one mile from its mouth, then moved down on its other side to the bank of the Great Kanawha and again pitched camp there. A heavy downpour of rain, continuing through the next day, delayed departure until Oct. 2.

During the final, five-day, 60-mile leg of the long journey here, the troops divided into two grand wings and marched with abundant military precautions through the woods along the north side of the Great Kanawha.

Two scouts, with a dozen supporting sergeants and with flankers to the right and left, moved well ahead to keep a sharp lookout for Indians.

Three columns, proceeding in parallel fashion, constituted the bulk of the grand design for forward movement. A central column of 400 men moved with a herd of beef cattle and remaining packhorses.

THERE WERE advance, rear and plain guards in the moving mass of men constituting the southern division of Dunmore's army. Action plans were ready for certain men to withstand a charge by the enemy, and others were assigned to execute pincer movements in the event of an attack from any direction.

Wearing their hunting outfits with fringed shirts dyed in various rich colors, their long, woolen leggings, their soft caps and moccasins, and with shot bags and powder horns hanging from their ornamental belts, the men cut a most unusual picture as they marched through the big woods.

Each man carried his flintlock, usually an English type musket or long rifle. Each carried his tomahawk and scalping knife. In keeping with the central purpose of the entire expedition, each was ready to kill an Indian.

The organized line of march sometimes moved across wide bottoms to the base of hills, where it was easier to cross streams. However, at some places, there was little room to march between rock cliffs and the river.

Somewhere within a two-mile area opposite Coal River, some of the troops went through what was described as an abandoned Indian fort, oval-shaped and about 100 yards long and with an eight-foot wide cellar full of water.

On the third day of the march, the troops were amazed at the sight of an area in which a hurricane or tornado had struck some years earlier.

The storm, sweeping the area clear of timber, came from the other side of the river and left a swath of destruction about two miles wide on both sides.

"The tops of the trees on this side all lie from the river and on the other side towards," Fleming said.

THREE DAYS AGO, when the marching Virginians reached this place that they chose to call Camp Point Pleasant; they found a letter in a hollow tree from their supreme commander Lord Dunmore.

It's believed that the message was brought by three scouts named, Simon Kenton, Simon Girty and Peter Parchment.

The message ordered Lewis and his men to join Dunmore and his forces at the mouth of the Big Hockhocking River, a tributary of the Ohio River about 65 miles upstream.

But the officers and troops here were in no mood to leave immediately. They had been led to believe earlier that they would meet his lordship here, and cross the Ohio River with him to fight the Indians.

Moreover, the men were tired, and the horses were worn out. It was considered wise to wait for the expected arrival of Col. William Christian with more men and supplies. It was thought unwise to vacate this strategic point and leave the frontier unprotected.

Lewis put some of those thoughts in a note and sent it to Dunmore.

Yesterday some men arrived in a canoe with another letter from his lordship, who expressed surprise that Lewis hadn't made his way to Fort Gower, the new structure at the mouth of the Big Hockhocking.

Lewis sent back a reply that he would start the march to Fort Gower as soon as all the troops, supplies and black powder arrived here.

One of the messengers from his lordship was an old Indian trader named William McCulloch. He hinted vaguely that Lewis might soon expect some hot work. He didn't explain.

The troops, including many Scotch Irish Presbyterians, attended religious services on this quiet Sunday. Their chaplain, the Rev. Mr. Terry, delivered a good sermon.

DESPITE ALL the peacefulness here, there are some minor problems. As a doctor, Fleming is concerned about some unsanitary conditions. He said the troops of each company soon will have a "necessary house," and he hopes they will use it.

There is much complaining among the men about the quality of beef. Matters haven't been helped by a Lewis order to kill the skinny cattle first.

Some of the men plan to go hunting for deer or other wild game tomorrow so they can have a change in their daily diets.

Sergeants James Robertson and Valentine Sevier want to kill a wild turkey so they can make some broth for the ailing James Shelby, son of Capt. Evan Shelby.

The 1,100-armed Virginians retired as darkness settled over this magnificent scenery. Guards were posted as usual.

Among the sleeping was the Commander-in-Chief Lewis. For him it was the evening of a special day. He was born in Ireland 54 years ago today.

CHAPTER 6

Cornstalk Wants to Skip Battle

EN ROUTE TO CAMP POINT PLEASANT, Va., Oct. 9,1774

His name is Keigh-tugh-qua, meaning the cornstalk or chief support of his people. He is known to Virginians as the Cornstalk Indian.

He is a large, graceful man whose whole appearance and manner suggest grandeur of the forest. His powerful oratory sweeps through an audience like a refreshing breeze through the trees.

Cornstalk is chief of the Shawnees and head of the Northwestern Confederated Tribes, including Delawares, Wyandots, Mingoes, Miamis, Ottawas, Illinois and others.

He is the supreme commander of 1,000 painted warriors who are crossing the Ohio River tonight with intent to murder an army of sleeping Virginians at the point between two waters.

Despite his position, his tested courage and leadership qualities, Cornstalk doesn't want to engage in this planned surprise attack. He feels that the time has come for the Indians to make peace with the white men.

AT A GRAND council meeting on Pickaway Plains in the Ohio Wilderness last month, Cornstalk twisted a hickory stick around his fingers as he talked. He said his easy way of handling the white was a lesson in how the Indians could have controlled the Virginians at some earlier time.

"But the circumstances are changed," he said. "Do you see that towering oak? There are the whites now grown strong, and we cannot uproot that monarch of the forest."

"The Long Knives (Virginians) are gathering to march against us. They have with them not only their long knives, but their long rifles too, and something tells me that we better make peace."

An unidentified Mingo chief didn't accept the elementary lesson. He called Cornstalk a coward.

"I am no coward," the supreme chief replied calmly. "My life, my acts, attest to my character. If my people resolve on war, I will myself lead them to the battlefield, and it shall be seen who the cowards are."

The mighty Cornstalk spoke in a melancholy, almost prophetic manner, as if he had some larger vision of impending doom of his race.

In earlier years he was something less than a peace-loving man. He was cruel and treacherous at times, a killer of women and children in two raids on Greenbrier River settlements 11 years ago.

Despite their present warlike attitude and their reputation as the fiercest tribe in the Northwest Territory, the Shawnees have had their yearnings for peace in the past.

WHEN THEY kicked Daniel Boone out of Can-tuc-kee land five years ago, they made their position clear. A Shawnee leader named Capt. Will told Boone and his party:

"Now brothers, go home and stay there. Don't come here any more, for this is the Indians' hunting ground, and all the animals, skins and furs are ours. If you are so foolish as to venture here again, you may be sure the wasps and yellow jackets will sting you severely."

Can-tuc-kee lands are a hot issue as land-hungry frontiersmen come across the Allegheny Mountains with hopes of moving down the Ohio River to the lush bluegrass country.

In a broad sense, a tremendous struggle is under way between two kinds of civilization: the Indians on one side with their hunting and fishing, and the whites on the other with their farming and commerce. Cornstalk symbolizes the Indian struggle with a curious blending of heroism and strength and some signs of futility and despair.

Cornstalk reigns over what has become known as the Shawnee capital, consisting of a complex of villages on a rich, oval grassland named Pick-away Plains and sometimes called Wilderness Garden.

THE PLAINS are above the bed of the Scioto River Valley and near the village of Chillicothe, which is in a vast area known as the Ohio Wilderness. It is something like 85 to 100 miles through the wilderness to the mouth of the Great Kanawha River, or the campsite of the Virginians.

There are four branches of the Shawnee tribes. They are called Piqua, men born in ashes; Kiskapoke, men of war; Mequacheke, fat men; and Chillicothe, dwellers in a permanent home.

The Kiskapoke obviously prevailed in the recent council sessions. Cornstalk clearly lost in his bid to make peace overtures to the whites. He nobly kept his pledge to lead the Shawnees and other tribes into battle. Delaware Indians, who have become friendly with the whites under Chief White Eyes, aren't included in the war party.

The broad plan of action for the Indian army is simple. It would wipe out the southern division of the Virginia militia under the command of Col. Andrew Lewis at the mouth of the Great Kanawha. It would then proceed against the northern division, commanded by Lord Dunmore and known to be moving far down the Ohio River from Pittsburgh.

THE INDIANS feel it is urgent to strike soon, before the two divisions meet. Fleet-footed warriors, following the high ridges, maintained excellent intelligence on the movements of the Lewis division as it marched from Camp Union to its encampment on the point between the Ohio and Kanawha Rivers.

The Dunmore division was observed by Indians as it moved across the northern neck of Virginia to Pittsburgh, then came down the Ohio River. This part of the army is reported to be encamped at least temporarily at the mouth of the Big Hockhocking on the Ohio. This location is about 65 miles upstream from the Lewis encampment.

If the Indians needed further information about the real intentions of Dunmore, somebody could have told them that it was in the newspaper. The *Maryland Journal* said Sept. 21:

"Lord Dunmore, we hear, with about 1.500 men was to march in a few days to the mouth of the New (Kanawha) River, where he is to be joined by Col. Lewis and Col. Preston, with a body of 1,200 or 1,500 men, their destination some of the Indian towns."

CORNSTALK rode on a horse as he led the warriors out of the Ohio Wilderness. Following him, also astride horses, were his brother, Silverheels; Chief Blue Jacket, Chief Black Snake, Chief Pucksinwah and his 18-year-old son, Chiksika. Pucksinwah's 6-year-old son, named Tecumseh, stayed at home.

In strategy sessions, the Indians considered two alternative plans: (1) Attacking the enemy as he crosses the Ohio River on his way to Indian villages and (2) ambushing the enemy after he makes the crossing.

But the alternative plans were abandoned, because the Indians were short on food and other supplies, and couldn't afford to wait for the Virginians to pick a date to cross the Ohio. The Indians proceeded with their original plan to cross at night and destroy the enemy at daybreak.

When darkness came today, the Indians treaded silently to the mouth of a small creek on the Ohio Wilderness side of the river, about three miles above the camp of the Virginians.

At this place the warriors took off all trinkets, ornaments and other unnecessary articles worn or attached to their sparse clothing. They hung the various items on bushes and assigned a small group to stand guard.

Then began the long and tedious loading of warriors, weapons and ammunition on 79 crude rafts, held together with grapevines.

THE WARRIORS are well supplied with powder, lead and guns, including flintlock muskets and rifles, in addition to tomahawks. Most of the military equipment and supplies reportedly were obtained in exchange for furs at trading posts in the Detroit area, Northwest Territory.

Far into the night, the sounds of wood and water, grunts and low talk of Indians were heard as they made the crossing. The general landing place is the site of "Old Shawnee Town" where the tribe lived until approximately 18 years ago. The town site is about a mile upstream from Old Town Creek.

The stealthy downriver advance against the Virginians isn't to begin until all warriors reach the other side. Scouting reports indicate that the terrain will be difficult for a large army to negotiate before daybreak tomorrow.

The ground, some of it quite marshy, is covered with high weeds, thickets of spicewood and other undergrowth. Fallen trees in various stages of decay will hinder progress if visibility is poor.

Growth of timber and foliage are said to be so dense in some areas they block the light of the moon and the stars. Only a sliver of the moon is shining tonight.

CHAPTER 7

EAR TO WATER — MYSTERIOUS. . .

FORT GOWER, Northwest Territory, Oct. 10, 1774

After completion of peace talks with Indians at Pittsburgh in mid-September, Lord Dunmore and 1,200 men descended the Ohio River to this place.

The fort is at the mouth of the Hockhocking River on the west bank of the Ohio, about 200 miles from Pittsburgh. It is a short distance downstream and on the opposite shore from the mouth of the Little Kanawha River.

Since coming here, his lordship has occasionally walked to the edge of the broad Ohio, put his ear to the water and listened intently. It is a rather mysterious practice.

To reach this place, his lordship and 700 men traveled in a flotilla of about 100 canoes, including some boats of larger dimensions, called pirogues. Another 500 men moved overland on the east bank of the Ohio.

ON THE WAY here, both sections of the army stopped at Fort Fincastle in Wheeling. Valentine Crawford, brother of the major in charge of overland operations, wrote about the arrival there in a letter to Col. George Washington.

His letter made reference to bullocks being herded along by foot soldiers. These were the beef cattle, slaughtered and cooked as needed for the main course in the daily fare on an expedition of this kind.

"I have just time to give you a line or two by Lord Dunmore's ex-press, to let you know how we go in this quarter with the Indian war."

Crawford wrote to Washington on Oct. 1:

"His lordship arrived here yesterday with about 1,200 men — 700 of whom came by water with his lordship — and 500 came under my brother — traveling by land with the bullocks. . . . His lordship has sent him with 500 men, 50 pack horses and 200 bullocks to the mouth of the Hockhocking River below the mouth of the Little Kanawha. His lordship is to go by water with the rest of the troops in a few days."

Maj. William Crawford led his men on a 110-mile march from Wheeling to a point opposite this location. Then the major, men and animals swam the Ohio.

Upon his arrival here, Crawford proceeded to construct a blockhouse and stockade just above the mouth of the Hockhocking. The new structure was named for the Earl of Gower in England, Dunmore's friend.

Dunmore lingered briefly at Wheeling and also paused for a while at the mouth of the Little Kanawha before making an appearance here. He had been given some assurance at Pittsburgh that Shawnee leaders might meet him downstream for peace talks.

The Delawares, Mohawks and others had talked in a friendly manner with Dunmore at Pittsburgh. But the fierce Shawnees weren't there.

ALONG WITH DUNMORE when he arrived here was his agent and confidant, Maj. John Connolly from Pittsburgh.

Still ranked next to Dunmore in the line of command is Col. Adam Stephen, an unusual man who has complained that this trip kept him from attending the first Continental Congress, which opened in Philadelphia Sept. 5.

In late August, Stephen wrote to R.H. Lee, a Virginia delegate to the Congress:

"Lord Dunmore orders me to the Ohio with his lordship to endeavor to put matters on a footing to establish a lasting peace with the brave natives. This prevents my attending the general Congress. The fate of America depends on your meeting, and the eyes of the European world are upon you, waiting the event."

With this statement, the colonel further wrote as if he expected some future conflict: "...let us be provided with arms and ammunition, and individuals may suffer, but the gates of hell cannot prevail against America."

Serving as scouts with Dunmore were Peter Parchment, Simon Girty and 19-year-old Simon Kenton.

KENTON HAD a narrow escape from Indians while hunting and trapping near the mouth of the Elk River in the spring of 1773. He and two partners were surprised by the savages while eating roasted turkey in their lean-to one rainy evening.

One of the partners was killed. Kenton and the other man escaped without guns, food or adequate clothing. The two made their way through backcountry to the mouth of the Great Kanawha, where they were rescued in an exhausted condition.

During a dull day or two here, some light entertainment was provided by Girty, his half-brother John Turner and Joseph and Thomas Nicholson.

The four, who had been prisoners of Indians, did some aboriginal war dances with accompanying songs. They kicked some firebrands around camp in lively Indian fashion, all to the delight of his lordship and his men.

To the disappointment of Dunmore, no Shawnees came to talk with him here. However, the royal Governor's forces were joined by friendly Delaware Chief White Eyes and a half-breed, John Mountour.

His lordship dispatched White Eyes to invite the Shawnees for a treaty. The Delaware chief quickly returned with an ominous message in figurative Indian style:

"Seven hundred warriors had gone southward to speak to the

army there, and they had been followed by another nation, that they would begin with the Virginians there in the morning, and their business would be over by breakfast."

The meaning was clear enough. The Shawnees would attack Lewis and expect to dispose of him and his men as a morning diversion before breakfast.

No one offered an explanation here as to why Dunmore didn't go immediately to Lewis' aid. But there has been much surmising about it.

Positively speaking, it is presumed that Dunmore knew he couldn't reach the mouth of the Great Kanawha in time to be of help. From this place, it is about 65 miles to Camp Point Pleasant, and less than half that distance as the crow flies.

A common presumption is that his lordship had supreme confidence in Lewis' superiority of numbers and quality of fighters. Moreover, while the Indians were engaged with Lewis, Dunmore would have an opportunity to push into the Ohio wilderness and attack their villages.

Negatively speaking, there was one report that Chief Blue Jacket of the Shawnees was seen talking with Dunmore in his tent here earlier and presumably told his lordship about plans to destroy the Lewis army. This was unconfirmed.

William Mann, a messenger, claims he was successful in urging Dunmore to hurry to Lewis at Camp Point Pleasant, but Connolly vetoed the idea.

One theory is that Dunmore was irked with Lewis because he didn't come to Fort Gower. Therefore, Dunmore felt no obligation to help Lewis.

This morning Dunmore and a young soldier named Abraham Thomas walked to the edge of the Ohio River. His lordship put his ear to the water, and said he thought he could hear guns roaring. He indicated to Thomas that he should also listen.

Thomas put his ear to the river surface and exclaimed, "I hear reports of musketry!" Later in the day, Dunmore was quoted as saying to Connolly: "By this time Lewis has had hot work."

CHAPTER 8

Indian Army Starts Attack At Daybreak

CAMP POINT PLEASANT, Va., Oct. 10, 1774

In the gray light of dawn today, an awesome army of Indians was seen coming through the woods about a mile from camp.

Scout James Mooney reported that he saw the savages near the Ohio River shore when he started deer hunting with a companion, Joseph Hughey.

The Indians fired twice at the hunters, killing Hughey on the spot. Mooney ducked into the woods and hightailed it back to camp.

The scout's report spread like wildfire through this camp of 1,100 men. Militiamen leaped to their feet, looked to their flints and powder, and were ready in minutes.

MANY OF the men gathered around Mooney in front of Capt. John Stuart's tent as the scout babbled the hair-raising story of the first sighting of Indians and first blood drawn in a big battle today.

Stuart jumped out of bed, ran out of his tent and demanded to know what was wrong. Mooney declared that he had seen Indians, so many of them that they covered five acres of ground when standing one beside another.

Col. Andrew Lewis took the news of the advancing enemy calmly as he smoked his pipe. Probably a large scouting party of Indians, he guessed. But he took no chances. He ordered the drummers to beat to arms.

He ordered his brother, Col. Charles Lewis, to lead 150 Augusta troops out the Kanawha River side of camp, and to move along the edge of Crooked Creek toward the enemy. He sent Col. Fleming out the Ohio River side with 150 Botetourt men.

Capt. John Dickinson, a veteran Indian fighter, paused and talked to a detachment of men before leading them into the field:

"Now my brave boys, screen yourselves from danger as much as possible and pull away — but you know just as well how to do it as I can tell you."

WHILE BATTLE preparations were under way, more hunters returned with reports that they had seen Indians. Any doubts about Mooney's story were dispelled.

Sergeants James Robertson and Valentine Sevier, who had been hunting turkey to make broth for the ailing James Shelby, said they saw a large body of Indians.

Robertson shot at one warrior, seen drinking from a stream. This was the first shot fired by the whites in the big battle today.

At about the same time, William Casey, 18, and others had walked a short distance from camp to collect horses hobbled out for feeding, when an Indian's gun roared nearby.

The youth was hit in the side and knocked down. He called out that he wasn't dead and urged the others to take trees, meaning to get behind trees. No additional shot was fired at that time. The Indian disappeared.

When Casey examined his wound, he found a lead ball just under the skin on his side. He easily extracted it. A further look showed that the ball lost its zing when it plowed through a shot pouch attached to his side.

MEANWHILE, under a rising October sun, detachments commanded by Lewis and Fleming moved briskly toward the enemy, now lurking behind trees, logs and bushes.

As the Lewis column entered a thicket of pa-paw bushes, the

Indians shot three times, then began heavy firing. Volley quickly followed volley as the Virginians returned the withering fire.

Instants later the Fleming column was brought under attack as it approached a pond near the Ohio River bank. Again the Virginia weapons talked back to the blazing guns fired by the Indians.

Heavy losses on both sides resulted from the early firing. But it was apparent that the Indians fared better from the exchange.

Two scouts on the front line were among the first Virginians killed. Ironically, one of them was Mooney.

Col. Charles Lewis was badly wounded, reportedly in the stomach, while standing on open ground and encouraging his men to advance. He handed his gun to a soldier and quit the field.

"I am wounded, but go on and be brave," he told his men.

Two men, Capt. John Murray and John Bailey, helped Lewis back to camp. The colonel was met by his brother, Col. Andrew Lewis, who remarked:

"I expected something fatal would befall you." "It is the fate of war," replied the wounded brother.

AS THE BATTLE raged, Fleming was hit twice in the left forearm, but he doggedly continued in the field. In a manner that suggested extraordinary presence of mind and coolness under fire, he urged his men to hold their positions or outflank the enemy.

But, after a third ball tore into his chest, he was helped from the field.

Fleming, a surgeon, noticed when he reached camp that a portion of his lung was protruding from his chest. With assistance, he returned the lung to its correct position.

After his wounds were dressed and, notwithstanding his own serious condition, Fleming visited Col. Charles Lewis in his tent. All signs were that Lewis' life was ebbing.

Strutting near the front of the Augusta column of men in the early action was John Frogg, a handsome young magistrate from Staunton, VA. In the colonial militia he was classified as a sutler, or supply officer.

He had a reputation as a fearless, generous, gallant man, with flairs for dramatic action and colorful clothes. On this battle occasion he wore a brilliant red jacket, which made him a prominent target. Indians could easily have marked him as a high-ranking officer.

He fell mortally wounded during an early phase of the battle. The Indian who shot him leaped for his scalp and perhaps also for his gay garment. Frogg, dramatic to the last, half arose to grapple with his foe.

At this point, noted Indian fighter William White watched for a chance and shot the warrior dead. He reloaded and fired again and again as more redskins approached with the same obvious purpose.

IN THE END, at least three dead Indians were stacked on the fallen Frogg. The shooting exhibition made White a hero among the militiamen.

Instinctively, as the general fighting intensified, the backwoodsmen broke ranks and started to take trees, bushes, logs and any other available cover in true Indian style. Alertly, the Indians seized their period of confusion to mount a sustained charge that drove the Virginians back about 200 yards.

As the Indians left their hiding places and charged into the open, they revealed themselves as painted and plumed warriors with all the trappings of war. Most were select young braves with athletic bodies, raven hair and glowering eyes. They fought as if vengeance were in their hearts.

They stalked the frontiersmen with guns, tomahawks and knives. The frontiersmen, wearing their fringed, colorful, homespun garbs, fought back tenaciously with the same types of weapons. There was much hand-to-hand fighting; survival depended on individual prowess.

All of the fighting was done amid war whoops, shouts, screams, jeers, groans and clatter. Guns cracked and roared, belched fire and smoke. Gunsmoke filled the air, burning eyes and nostrils.

Cornstalk

Above the din of battle, beside the mingled flowing waters amid the splendor of the Virginia hills on this bright October morning, was heard the voice of the mighty Cornstalk:

"Oui-shi-cat-to-oui! oui-shi-cat-to-oui!" (be strong, be strong).

CHAPTER

FAITHFUL SERVANT SAVES SCALP

CAMP POINT PLEASANT, Va., Oct. 10, 1774

While Indians were forcing back Virginians in their continuing big battle this morning, Col. John Field was ordered into action with 200 more militiamen.

The dashing Field and his men made a strong move in support of the Augusta wing of the Virginians and caused the enemy to retreat a few steps.

THE COLONEL, who had a strong desire to wreak vengeance upon the Indians for the capture of his son, continued to advance with rare determination.

Knowing that other officers had fallen as they fought in the open earlier this morning, he moved cautiously from tree to tree.

As he stood against one big tree, an Indian jeered from a distance on his left side. Field wheeled and prepared to shoot. When he turned his back, two Indians lurking on the right shot him dead.

Several Indians surged toward the fallen Field in quest of his scalp. But a huge dark man popped out of nowhere and powered his way among them to claim the body of his master.

This was the colonel's faithful mulatto servant, a man of extraordinary strength. He knocked down one savage, hoisted the body of the colonel on his shoulder and ran with it to camp.

Other Indians, seemingly showing respect for the courageous dark man and his burden, withheld their fire.

THE VIRGINIANS, demoralized by the death of Field, heard more bad news later in the day. The popular Col. Charles Lewis, wounded in the early action, died in his tent at noon.

Lewis is said to have died in the arms of Charles Simms, a commissary officer. Simms quoted these last words of Lewis: "I sent one of them to eternity."

By losing the services of Lewis, Fleming and Field through death or disability, the Virginians in fact lost their second, third and fourth officers, respectively, in the line of command. The disability of Fleming, a surgeon as well as an officer, is regarded as a double loss.

Col. Andrew Lewis, the commander-in-chief and brother of the fallen Charles, continued to direct the Virginians from camp headquarters.

The 200 men brought in as reinforcements raised the total of Virginians in action to 500, against an estimated 1,000 Indians. As more troops were added, the number of participating Virginians exceeded 700, or about two thirds of the 1,100 men in camp.

ALL CAPTAINS eventually saw action, except Alexander McClanahan, who remained on guard duty, and John Lewis, the commander-in-chief's 24-year-old son who was placed in charge of defense of the camp and construction of breast-works.

Trees were felled by a reserve corps for use as barriers in the event of an attempted invasion of the camp.

Battle lines stretched approximately 1 1/4 mile through the woods by late morning. At no point were the lines more than 20 yards apart. Bloody hand-to-hand contests, featuring use of knives and tomahawks, dominated the general battle scene.

Capt. Evan Shelby, a 54-year-old woodsman and hunter, became the new commander in the field. His son, Lt. Isaac Shelby, was named leader of the father's company.

"LET US move forward, my brave boys, right and left and drive them," the younger Shelby said when orders came to advance the Botetourt line. He ran well ahead of his men and threw himself among the large, projecting roots of an elm tree. A soldier dived for the same cover, but was dead on arrival, a victim of an Indian sharpshooter.

Action continued in extremely hot fashion around noon as Capt. Shelby and his men effected a small advance. Peals of musketry, mingled with whoops, shouts, thumps, thuds and the general clatter of battle.

Richard Burk, a droll Irishman, enjoyed a comfortable position behind a log during a sizzling phase of the action. He put his hat on the end of a ramrod and raised it slightly above the log.

When an Indian fired, the hat disappeared. To complete his act, Burk kicked and struggled on the ground and gave his antagonist a glimpse of a backwoodsman in death agony. Burk had his musket ready when the Indian came to collect his scalp. He killed two Indians in the same manner.

"Well, I believe I've earned my dinner," the undisciplined Burk said at noon. He ran from the battlefield, refreshed himself in camp and returned to the firing line.

During the time of much sound and fury, William Clendenin found a fanciful Indian cap and quickly thrust it in the bosom of his shirt. Later he was staggered by the impact of a lead ball that struck the concealed cap but wounded him only slightly.

As he rolled with the tremendous punch that might have killed him, a popeyed Indian arose from behind a log and waited for his intended victim to fall. Clendenin collected his wits, whipped his gun to his shoulder and killed the Indian.

In the redskin's shot pouch, Clendenin found five fresh scalps. It dawned on him that an Indian's cap had saved his own scalp.

William Bryan was credited with saving the life of Thomas Lewis, son of the commander-in-chief and youngest brother of Capt. John. Bryan yelled when he saw an Indian draw a bead on young Lewis, who dodged and received only a graze on the bridge of his nose. Lewis turned, fired pointblank at the Indian and sent him sprawling with a mortal wound.

WILLIAM STEPHEN, 14, was the youngest white soldier killed today. John McKinney, 15, was wounded badly. Capt. John Dickinson, the veteran Indian fighter who had warned his men about the importance of taking cover, was listed among the wounded.

George Cameron, assistant commissary officer and enthusiastic soldier, grabbed his gun and insisted on going to meet the enemy when the men first organized for battle. But his brother, Lt. Charles Cameron, persuaded him to remain on duty in camp.

When George Cameron heard the thunder of guns and the discouraging reports on progress of the battle, he knew that his brother was in danger. He ran into the thick of the battle and did very well for a time, but the Indians killed him.

Lt. Matthew Bracken was on a spying mission across the Ohio River when he heard the sounds of battle. He returned to camp and upbraided some of the men for remaining behind logs like cowards. He strode on open ground and soon was shot down.

A 7-foot scout named James Fowler also was across the Ohio when the action began. It is said that he entered a shallow part of the river at low ebb, watched his step carefully, waded to camp side and warmly participated in the conflict.

Mighty Chief Cornstalk's loud voice, soaring above the battle noises, could be heard throughout the morning:

"Oui-shi-cat-to-oui! Oui-shi-cat-to-oui!" (be strong, be strong).

Other Cornstalk commands were interpreted to mean, "lie low" and "shoot well."

DRIVE THE WHITE DOGS IN. . .

CAMP POINT PLEASANT, Va. Oct. 10, 1774

The strategy of Chief Cornstalk soon became apparent today in the battle at the point where the two rivers meet.

He planned to drive the "Long Knives" (Virginians) into the rivers like cattle. While he moved up and down the battle line, yelling, "Be strong, lie low and shoot well," Indian children and squaws stood on far sides of the rivers and yelled something else.

AMID THE BATTLE roar, the faint cries from across the waters were hard to hear. But Jacob Persinger and others who had been prisoners of Indians understood this chant: *Drive the white dogs in, drive the white dogs in.*

Obviously, the odd assortment of Indians on the opposite shores had been stationed there to clobber any white soldier who might try to save his scalp by swimming a river.

The strategy almost certainly would have worked if a few militiamen hadn't gone deer hunting at the crack of dawn today.

The hunters spoiled plans for the 1,000-man Indian army to creep up on 1,100 Virginians and murder them in their sleep or chase them into the rivers.

TWO SHOTS, marking the start of the battle today, were fired by the Indians when they spied two hunters before sunrise. One hunter was killed, but the other made his escape to spread the alarm.

The first shot was fired by Elinipsico, son of Cornstalk. The second, following quickly was fired by Tavenor Ross, a young white man adopted by the Indians. Ross was credited with the kill.

Shawnee Chief Pucksinwah was by far the most prominent Indian who fell in battle today. He was the father of a six-year-old son named Tecumseh and an 18-year-old son named Chiksika.

Chiksika fought by his father's side until shortly before noon when the chief was hit in the chest by a ball from a Virginia musket. It is said that, as the chief lay dying in Chiksika's arms, he asked his oldest son to take care of Tecumseh and to uphold the high traditions of the family.

SILVERHEELS, brother of Cornstalk, fought until he collapsed with exhaustion. He had been weakened by a chest wound received in a skirmish prior to today's battle.

Nonhelema, the giant sister of Silverheels and Cornstalk, pulled her exhausted brother out of range of the flying lead balls. She was the only woman on the battlefield.

Cornstalk whipped one man and tomahawked another for acts of cowardice today. Reportedly, he applied the tomahawk to a Mingo chief who earlier accused Cornstalk of being afraid to fight.

During the battle, Cornstalk kept a close watch on the chief, discovered him in the act of skulking from danger and promptly cleaved his skull.

RENEGADE ROSS further endeared himself to his Shawnee brothers with demonstrations of battlefield cunning and valor.

Once, when he retired briefly from the battle scene to unchoke his gun, he saw two prominent Indians fall successively without reasonable explanation. He looked around carefully and spotted a young Cherokee as he was getting off a shot at his third victim.

Without hesitation, Ross ran to the Cherokee and bashed his head with a war club. This impulsive act caused commotion among the Indians.

They viewed Ross with suspicion until they determined that three warriors had been shot from behind and that the Cherokee was in position to shoot all three. Then they warmly commended their white brother.

NO ONE EXPLAINED why the Cherokee, reared mostly by Shawnees, chose to shoot his fellow warriors in the back while they were fighting Long Knives.

At another time, Ross observed that puffs of gunsmoke were emerging regularly from a clump of bushes. He peered into the bushes, saw the dim outline of a long knife, and silenced him with one peal of musketry.

Ross was one of four adopted white men who fought with the Indians. The others were Blue Jacket, White Wolf and George Collett.

Collett repeatedly yelled during the battle, "Fight on, fight on. We'll soon whip them all." His body was found by his brother, Thomas, a Virginian militiaman.

WHITE WOLF, 33, named John Ward until Shawnee Indians captured him when he was a small boy, upheld his reputation as a sharpshooter today. He waited patiently between shots and fired at heads as they might emerge from behind trees or logs.

One of the Virginians hit between the eyes as he looked over a log, was Capt. James Ward. 54, who had yearned for vengeance against the Shawnees for capture of his son.

Was the fatal shot fired by White Wolf? No one knows.

Blue Jacket fired his flintlock twice, and then resorted to the ancient art of shooting with bow and arrows until his quiver was empty.

For the remainder of the battle, the muscular Blue Jacket sought close combat with the Virginians as he moved about with a tomahawk in one hand and a knife in the other.

BLUE JACKET, whose name was Marina-duke Van Swearingen

when he roamed the woods as a boy and wanted to be captured, killed five or more men today. He killed one Indian who showed signs of cowardice.

Indians frequently took occasion during the battle to taunt the whites with smart remarks and questions.

"Well learn you to shoot." they said. The Long Knives repeatedly demonstrated superior shooting skill. But the Indians were best at avoiding balls by keeping under cover. "Why don't you whistle now?" the Indians asked in alluding to the fifes of the Virginians.

THEY SAID THEY would have 1,100 warriors to match the 1,100 Virginians in the battle next day and perhaps 2,000 Indians the following day.

They made merriment about a treaty of some kind. How would they know anything about a treaty? What did they mean? The questions weren't answered.

By noon it was apparent that the Cornstalk strategy had failed. The camp hadn't been invaded. Not a single soldier had been driven into the river.

As lines of fighting stabilized, the battle settled into a pattern that is most unusual for Indians. They like to outnumber, overwhelm and outflank the enemy with shrieking warriors get it all over with and go home.

Now, with no nearby source of food or a supply line, they would have to win quickly or return to their villages or hunting grounds for refreshments. They had to conquer the Long Knives or retreat to eat.

CHAPTER 11

LONG, SLOW RETREAT BEGUN BY INDIANS

CAMP POINT PLEASANT, Va., Oct. 10, 1774

The fierce, daylong battle between red warriors and white frontiersmen ended just after sundown today.

The turning point came at about 1 p.m. when gunfire subsided, and the Indians began a long, slow, strategic retreat from the Virginians.

Trees, bushes, old logs, embankments and the general terrain beside the Ohio River were used to great advantage by the Indians as they moved backward under all available cover.

They put up occasional shots to discourage immediate pursuit and to shield their efforts to remove the dead and wounded.

UNTIL about 4 p.m. there was a genuine lull in the battle. Shooting almost ceased as the two sides stared and cursed at each other. Indians clearly showed that they had lost their enthusiasm for fighting.

At this time, Col. Andrew Lewis decided on a diversionary tactic to hasten the retreat. He pulled veteran captains John Stuart, Matthew Arbuckle and George Matthews, and Lt. Isaac Shelby from the front, and gave them specific orders.

Accordingly, they dropped behind the Kanawha River bank with a detachment of men and moved upstream a quarter of a mile to the mouth of Crooked Creek.

They proceeded up the eastern edge of the creek with intentions of firing at the enemy from the rear. Although they were discovered before the mission was accomplished, they succeeded in dislodging the Indians.

PERHAPS thinking that reinforcements had arrived for the enemy, the Indians swiftly vacated the premises. Although they released a low yell, as if they were about to fight again, they extended their retreat to Old Town Creek, about two miles up the Ohio River.

At this point, the Indians were well protected by heavy undergrowth. They chose to make a stand right there. "Come on," they shouted at the advancing Virginians.

But the Virginians, suspecting a trick, chose to halt their advance. They maintained a quiet battle line until nightfall.

The Indians disappeared into the night. Scouts reported that they were last seen going back across the Ohio.

The final withdrawal of the Indians was regarded as a fine display of generalship on the part of Chief Cornstalk.

Why did the Indians lose the battle under a chief of his caliber? One of the reasons given is that they failed to keep their guns in top condition. Another is that too many braves recklessly exposed themselves to danger in the hope of getting prize scalps or plunder.

When all the firing had ceased today, a voice was heard on the darkening Ohio River shore: "You may come out now, Andy. All is safe." It was the voice of an old Dutchman named Andrew Kishioner Sr., calling out to his son, Andrew Jr.

The two, attached to the Virginia Militia, left camp after the first alarm of approaching Indians and spent the day under piles of driftwood.

At day's end the weary army of backwoodsmen returned to camp, which has been turned into a crude field hospital, practically without medicine or skilled attendants.

Col. William Fleming, rated as the best surgeon, remains among the critically wounded.

Poultices of slippery elm bark are applied to wounds. Broth, made from beef or wild game, is offered as nourishment.

Groans of the wounded pierce the night in a manner that is heartrending to other officers and men.

At nightfall the official count of dead frontiersmen stood at 46, including nine commissioned officers. More were expected to die. Counts of the wounded varied from 80 to 92.

No reliable information is available on how many Indians were killed. Officers insist that the total must be higher than that of the Virginians.

INDIANS were seen putting many of their dead in the Ohio River. They also scalped some of their own to keep Virginians from getting them. Traditionally, Indians don't like to leave their dead for the enemy to mutilate.

Officers counted 18 to 20 scalps of Indians taken during the day. They were certain the Indians got only a few scalps of Virginians, and those only from stragglers away from the main battle scene.

Left on the battlefield, as the Indians hastily departed were 23 guns, 80 blankets, 27 tomahawks and several skins, shot pouches, powder horns and war clubs.

Earlier today Lewis sent a messenger to meet Col. William Christian, ordering him to make a forced march to Camp Point Pleasant.

Christian already was en route to camp from the mouth of Elk River with 220 men in a convoy of cattle and supplies. When met by the messenger about 15 miles from here, Christian and most of his men left the convoy and continued toward camp with all possible speed. They reached here about midnight.

Arrival of Christian and his men, including captains William Campbell, James Harrod and John Floyd, brought new feelings of hope and security throughout this military establishment.

A heavy guard was placed around camp tonight. The password is "victory." But some think it is a hollow victory in view of the heavy losses of courageous men.

Thus ended a long day of battle from sunup to sundown, followed by a little happiness and much misery in the night at this camp on *Tu-Endie-Wei* (Indian lingo for a point between two waters).

Figures Give Warped View

CAMP POINT PLEASANT, Va., Oct. 17, 1774

Seventeen dressed scalps of Indians hang on a pole here. Bodies of at least 46 Virginians are buried here.

Those are basic figures about the Battle of Point Pleasant, fought a week ago today. But officers say the figures give a warped view of the facts.

They believe the Indians had a much higher death toll than the Virginians. The reason there aren't more scalps on the pole is that the Indians carried many of their dead off the battlefield and dumped them in the river or concealed them elsewhere.

Indians also scalped some of their own men when they reached the bodies first. Many saplings were chopped down by Indians for use in transporting the dead and wounded from the field.

CLAIMS OF SOLID victory continue to be voiced here by members of the southern division of Lord Dunmore's army, commanded by Col. Andrew Lewis. After all, the Indians retreated, and they didn't return.

Col. William Fleming said on the day after the battle: "Hearty thanks is returned to the brave officers and men who distinguished themselves in the battle of yesterday, by whose gallant behavior a victory under God was obtained."

He added later: "Never did the Indians stick closer to it nor behave bolder. Let me add I believe the Indians never had such a scourging from the English before."

In this atmosphere of victory, Lewis and about 1,150 men are preparing to cross the Ohio River and march toward Shawnee villages today.

Lewis is acting under orders from Lord Dunmore, who said he will meet with the colonel on the way to the Shawnee homes on the Pickaway Plains, deep inside the Ohio wilderness. The designated meeting place is a high ridge this side of the Indian villages, about 85 miles from here.

ORDERS TO PROCEED to Pickaway Plains actually were received by Lewis Oct. 13. But he didn't comply for a few days because of duties he considered mandatory here.

The work included burying the dead, bringing in cattle abandoned on a trail beside the Great Kanawha River, rounding up horses stampeded by the battle, building a storehouse and breast-works, reorganizing the army because of the loss of top officers and receiving additional supplies brought from the mouth of Elk River by Capt. Thomas Slaughter.

Many officers and men used their spare time during the past week to express their views about the battle in letters to relatives, friends and military associates.

"I gladly embrace this opportunity to acquaint you that we are all three yet alive through God's mercies," Lt. Isaac Shelby wrote to his Uncle John. The three included the lieutenant, his father, Capt. Evan Shelby, and brother, James Shelby.

His letter contained this bad news: "Five men in Daddy's company were killed." And this comment on the horrors of battle: "Sometimes the hideous cries of the enemy and the groans of our wounded men lying around was enough to shudder the stoutest heart."

FLEMING, A SURGEON, described his wounds: "I received three balls on the left line, two struck my left arm below the elbow. A third entered my breast about three inches below my left nipple and is lodged somewhere in the chest."

The colonel, who had assured his wife earlier that he would be spared in battle, wrote to her after receiving his wound:

"I praise the Almighty I did not fall, and had strength with assistance to reach my tent. I bless God my wounds are in a good way."

He made this general comment about the battle "And though many brave men lost their lives, yet I hope in its consequences, it will be a general good to the country, and the engagement will be long remembered to the memory and honor of those who purchased the victory by their deaths."

Capt. John Floyd, who arrived here after the battle, made complimentary and uncomplimentary remarks about the officers who participated in the action:

"Many of the officers with a great deal of courage behaved like heroes, while others lurked behind and could by no means be induced to advance to the front."

COL. ANDREW LEWIS wrote an address to the Augusta County regiment in tribute to his brother, Col. Charles Lewis, who was killed while leading the regiment into battle here.

"In losing him I have lost the best of brothers," he wrote. "A regard to his memory would be inducement enough to me to treat the brave officers and troops of Augusta with all tenderness and just marks of esteem."

The commanding officer's report of the battle was incorporated in a letter written by Col. Waltham Christian to Col. William Preston.

Christian, who arrived here with 220 men about midnight Oct. 10, several hours after the daylong battle ended, has been engaged in mopping up operations and related activities since that time.

Before receipt of the new orders to go into Indian country, Christian had hoped that Lord Dunmore would come here to provide assistance in taking care of the wounded. There had been earlier indications that his lordship might come down the Ohio River from Fort Gower.

During a tour of the camp two days ago, Christian reached the conclusion that many of the wounded might die. "There are many shot in two places," he said. "One in particular I observed with two bullets, and some with three."

"They are really in deplorable condition. Bad doctors, few medicines, nothing proper to eat make it still worse."

The death count still stands officially at 46 Virginians. But it's understood that this number already has been exceeded and may continue to grow. The total of wounded, originally about 90, also is increasing.

During the battle, the militiamen fought as two major formations — the Augusta and Botetourt lines. In addition to Col. Charles Lewis, the dead in the Augusta line included Col. John Field, Capt. Samuel Wilson, Lt. Hugh Allen and 18 privates.

Among the dead in the Botetourt line were Captains John Murray, Robert McClanahan, James Ward and Thomas Buford; Lieutenants Mathew Bracken and Edward Goldman, Ensign Jonathan Cundiff and 17 privates.

There is much activity today as men complete the roundups of beef cattle and packhorses for the trip across the Ohio River and into Indian Territory. Each man is to be allotted a half-pound of powder, 1 1/2 pound of lead balls or bullets and a five-day supply of beef.

About 118 beef cattle are to swim across the river and move with the 1,150 men. Sixty strong horses have been selected to carry a 10-day supply of flour.

Fleming is to remain in charge of 278 men here. Lewis gave him these instructions:

"Your principal duty will be to secure this camp from the attack of the enemy should any appear and make the works that are so far carried on as complete as you can."

CHAPTER

PEACE WITH THE INDIANS. . .

CAMP CHARLOTTE, Northwest Territory, Oct. 25, 1774

Peace with the Indians was announced here today by Lord Dunmore. At the same time his lordship said thanks and goodbye to Col. Andrew Lewis and his men.

Thus dismissed, the Virginia militiamen turned their faces toward the Ohio River and began marching with thoughts of home. Peace, coming 15 days after the Battle of Point Pleasant, was attained in an improvised conference center here at the edge of Pickaway Plains. The site is within a few miles of the main Shawnee village of Chillicothe.

Agreement to bury the bloody hatchet was reached after several days of negotiations that featured the eloquence of one Indian chief at the conference table and another chief who explained why he wouldn't come.

The two splendid Indians are Shawnee Chief Cornstalk and Mingo Chief Logan. Either could be called "Demosthenes of the Forest."

LORD DUNMORE is chief negotiator for the Virginians. He and 1,200 men arrived here Oct. 17 after a six-day trip from Fort Gower at the mouth of the Big Hockhocking on the Ohio River.

During the march up the Hockhocking River Valley and over the highlands into the Scioto River Valley, Dunmore was at his best as a man of wit and humor who enjoyed association with soldiers. He marched with the men and carried his own knapsack.

On the evening of Oct. 16, about 15 miles from Shawnee villages, Dunmore and his men were approached by a white man waving a flag of truce.

The man identified himself as Matthew Eliot, a trader who said the Indians were ready to make peace. Dunmore agreed to start negotiating upon his arrival here the next day. A small pole building was constructed for his headquarters.

On a peeled section of a large white oak tree nearby, Dunmore wrote in red chalk: "Camp Charlotte." The name suggests two women in his life: Lady Dunmore and the Queen of England.

Around the conference table gathered Dunmore, the presiding officer; Maj. John Connolly, secretary; Capt. John Gibson and Thomas Nicholson, interpreters; Col. Adam Stephen; Maj. William Crawford; Capt. George Rogers Clark and others. They waited for the Indians.

IN A SENSE, the Indians came a long way to this conference. Before the Battle of Point Pleasant, Chief Cornstalk advised against war. Later he was angry about the battle results and at the Indians who didn't agree with him in the first place.

When the Indians held their own council after the battle, Cornstalk demanded, "What will you do now? The Big Knives (Virginians) are pressing upon us with two powerful armies, and we shall all be killed. Now you must fight or we are undone." No answer.

"Then let us kill our women and children and fight until not one shall be left to tell the story of the once proud Shawnees," he declared with grim sarcasm. Silence.

"Then I will go and make peace," Cornstalk declared as he sank his tomahawk in the central post of the council house.

The warriors grunted agreement all around.

On Oct. 18, when the peace conference opened with Dunmore and his officers here, Cornstalk appeared with half moons painted on his cheeks, a beaded ornament on his forehead and silver rings in his ears. He wore a topknot with red feathers.

With him were his sister, the tall Nonhelema, called the "Grenadier Squaw," and her graceful daughter, Fanny. Both rode fine horses with elegant saddles.

DURING THE CONFERENCE, Cornstalk spoke eloquently and loudly. He vividly sketched the proud history of the Shawnees, compared to their present fallen condition. He charged that the Virginians started the war.

While negotiations were in progress, Lewis and 1,150 men made their way through the Ohio wilderness from Point Pleasant, Va.

Moving in a northwesterly direction, they came into this area by way of the Scioto River and Salt Creek valleys and thence to the bank of Kinnickinnick Creek about 15 miles from here.

At that point yesterday, an Indian named White Fish brought a message from Dunmore, saying that a treaty was in the making and ordering Lewis to make camp. However, Lewis' army had been fired on that morning, and he chose to look for a safer campsite. His guide got lost and moved the whole army to a site on Congo Creek, entirely too close to the villages.

It was a frightening time for the Shawnees. They seemed caught in a pincer movement. With Dunmore's Northern division of 1,200 men already there, the approach of Lewis's southern division of 1,150 men was an ominous prospect.

Cornstalk and the other chiefs fled to the villages to protect the women and children, leaving the formalities of peacemaking not quite finished.

Dunmore was upset. He began to fear that Lewis' men would insist on attacking the villages.

SO WITH about 50 men, including the friend, Delaware Chief White Eyes, Dunmore rode late yesterday to Lewis' camp, about six miles from Camp Charlotte. Enroute, White Eyes asked a simple question: "Can one big man stop another big man?"

Dunmore seemed satisfied with Lewis' explanations, which included assurance that the villages wouldn't be attacked. The two leaders made their peace.

But much bitterness remains among Lewis men. They feel that they have been denied a chance to have another crack at the Indians.

Today his lordship requested to be introduced to Lewis' officers. He thanked them for their gallantry and assured them that the Shawnees had agreed to all terms of the peace treaty.

He ordered return of Lewis and his men to Camp Point Pleasant and from thence to their homes.

The peace terms, subject to change next year at a Pittsburgh conference, are overwhelmingly favorable to the Virginians. They provide that the Indians:

Deliver all prisoners, surrender all Negroes taken from white persons, return all stolen horses and valuable effects, stop hunting on the southeastern side of the Ohio River, deliver certain hostages and follow the King's regulations.

White persons aren't to hunt on the Indian side of the Ohio.

MINGO CHIEF LOGAN didn't attend the peace conference. Interpreter John Gibson found him under a nearby spreading elm tree and urged his attendance.

Chief Logan

Logan, who had just returned from a bloody foray in which he took many scalps in revenge for the murder of his family last April, burst into tears and uttered this speech:

"I appeal to any white man to say, if ever he entered Logan's cabin hungry, and he gave him not meat; if ever he came cold and naked, and he clothed him not." During the course of the last long and bloody war, Logan remained idle in his cabin, an advocate for peace.

"Such was my love for the whites, that my countrymen pointed as they passed, and said, 'Logan is the friend of the white men.' I had even thought to have lived with you, but for the injuries of one man." Col. Cresap, then last spring, in cold blood, and unprovoked, murdered all the relations of Logan, not sparing even my women and children.

'There runs not a drop of my blood in the veins of any living creature. This called on me for revenge. I have sought it: I have killed many: I have glutted my vengeance. For my country I rejoice at the beams of peace.

"But do not harbor a thought that mine is the joy of fear. Logan never felt fear. He will not turn on his heel to save his life. Who is there to mourn for Logan? Not one."

CHAPTER 14

DUNMORE GETS HERO'S WELCOME

WILLIAMSBURG, Va., Dec. 24, 1774

Lord Dunmore received a hero's welcome upon his return to the Governor's Palace in the colonial capital here Dec. 4.

His joy was heightened when he learned that Lady Dunmore gave birth to a daughter on the previous day. The royal couple named her Virginia in honor of the colony.

Congratulatory messages on his declared victory over the Indians and the birth of his daughter were sent to his lordship by the 12-member council of state, the faculty of William and Mary College, the mayor and other officials on behalf of Williamsburg citizens.

ALL OF THE MESSAGES commented on the fatigue and danger which his lordship underwent in commanding a successful five-month expedition against the Indians and bringing them to peace terms.

Notwithstanding all of the bouquets, Dunmore hasn't occupied a bed of roses since the day of his return when he found a scorching letter on his desk from Lord Dartmouth.

Dartmouth, the English secretary of state for the colonies, expressed his displeasure with some aspects of the frontier activity of Dunmore and his agent, Maj. John Connolly.

In the letter dated Sept. 8, Dartmouth said it was his

intelligence that some of the hostility of the Indians was caused by unprovoked ill treatment initiated by Connolly.

The letter contained other criticism, sought clarifying information and ended with this dark threat, bearing directly on Dunmore's future as an English official: "Such steps may be taken as the king's dignity and justice shall dictate."

A SECOND LETTER from Dartmouth expressed extreme displeasure with Dunmore's violation of the limited land grant policy in the royal proclamation of 1763.

Today, Christmas eve, Dunmore wrote a long, tedious letter to Dartmouth and attempted to explain his military and peace-making actions during the past few months.

In closing, he noted that shocking circumstances concerning the war may have produced good effects by impressing the power of white people on Indians.

"And there is reason to believe it has extinguished the rancor which raged so violently in our people against the Indians, and I think there is a greater probability that the scenes of distress will never be renewed, than ever was before," he added.

Practically speaking, the triumphant return of his lordship to the city marked the end of the so-called Dunmore's War. Essentially, it began last spring when Indian uprisings and aggressions by Virginians reached fever pitch.

THE MURDER of Mingo Chief Logan's family last April 30 was one of the main turning points. Dunmore later called out the militia and left for the frontier July 10.

Dunmore was no closer than 66 miles upstream and 28 miles across the country to the only real battle in his war — the Battle of Point Pleasant fought between Virginians and Indians on Oct. 10.

But he ordered and participated in the organization of an army of 2,700 men, led its northern division and served as chief negotiator at a successful peace conference. He marched several hundred miles with his men, over mountains, through the woods and across streams.

After completion of peace negotiations at Camp Charlotte in the Ohio Wilderness Oct. 30, Dunmore and the northern division of 1,200 men returned to Fort Gower at the confluence of the Big Hockhocking and Ohio rivers.

On that date, at least partially because the Continental Congress had been meeting in Philadelphia Sept. 5 to Oct. 26, some of the men thought it would be appropriate to say something about the grievances of British America. One officer, believed to be Col. Adam Stephen, said:

> "Gentlemen, having now concluded the campaign, by the assistance of Providence, with honor and advantage to the colony, it only remains that we should give our country the stronger assurance that we are ready at all times, to the utmost of our power, to maintain and defend her rights and privileges."

Then followed a curious resolution, pledging allegiance to the King, defense of liberty and respect for Dunmore, as follows:

> "Resolved that we will bear the most faithful allegiance to his majesty, King George III, while his majesty delights to reign over a brave and free people; that we will at the expense of life and everything dear and valuable, exert ourselves in the support of his crown and the dignity of the British Empire.'
>
> "But as the love of liberty and attachment to the real interests and just rights of America outweigh every other consideration, we resolve that we will exert every power within us for the defense of American liberty and for the support of her just rights and privileges, not in any precipitous, riotous and tumultuous manner, but when regularly called forth by the unanimous voice of our countrymen.'
>
> "Resolved that we entertain the greatest respect for his excellency, the right honorable Lord Dunmore, who

> commanded the expedition against the Shawnees and who, we are confident, underwent the great fatigue of this singular campaign from no other motives than the true interests of the country.'

THE RESOLUTION was signed by Benjamin Ashby, clerk, by order and in behalf of the whole corps.

From Fort Gower, some of the men returned home by way of the Little Kanawha Valley. But most men in the northern and southern divisions of the Dunmore army moved homeward in small groups over the same routes by which they came.

Dunmore assigned garrisons of 25 men at Fort Fincastle in Wheeling and 100 men at Fort Dunmore in Pittsburgh.

Capt. William Russell was placed in charge of 50 men at Point Pleasant. He began construction of Fort Blair there.

Col. William Fleming, the seriously wounded commander of the Botetourt County regiment was in charge of Camp Point Pleasant during the earlier peace conference.

He continued to keep a record of routine activities at camp, including one notation that someone caught an 89-pound catfish, 10 inches between the eyes, two feet and four inches around the head, and four feet and 10 inches long.

On Oct. 31, after peace was reported, Fleming left camp in a canoe on the Great Kanawha River with Capt. John Dickinson and four watermen. On the fourth day he arrived at the mouth of Elk River, where he rounded up packhorses for the overland homeward journey.

He proceeded up the north bank of the Great Kanawha to Kelly's Creek, went up the creek valley, proceeded through the backcountry, and traveled Gauley Mountain on the Augusta Path.

In the mountainous area it snowed 11/2 inch on Nov. 8. On the night of Nov. 9, it was very cold on a mountaintop, and the camping ground was "bad and stony." When he reached Meadow River, Fleming suddenly realized that his wounds were inflamed and that he was running a fever.

His condition grew worse as he neared the Camp Union area at the Great Levels on the Greenbrier River, where the Dunmore army had organized its southern division more than two months ago. Friends met him in that area and provided some assistance.

"I got bleeding [in] the arm," he said. "My wounds were much inflamed. The arm swelled greatly and the most violent, shooting, flying pains in my hands and fingers."

But Fleming was feeling better by the time he crossed the main ridge of the Allegheny Mountains Nov. 17. Five days later he reached his home named Belmont.

"Reached home safely," Fleming recorded in his journal Nov. 22. "Just three months gone, praise be to God."

CHAPTER 15

A CENTURY PASSES. . .

POINT PLEASANT, W. Va., Oct. 10, 1874

Marching to the beat of muffled drums, a company of West Virginia University cadets proceeded down Main Street here today.

In background, the Mason County Court House bell tolled. A church bell chimed in.

The cadets escorted a metallic coffin containing the bones of some Virginia militimen who died in the Battle of Point Pleasant 100 years ago today.

The bones were exhumed from scattered graves yesterday under supervision of Dr. A. R. Barbee. They were placed in the coffin and loaded on a horse-drawn hearse for removal to an appropriate burial site.

THE PROCESSION today moves to the point of ground between the Great Kanawha and Ohio Rivers. On that hallowed place, the bones were recommitted to earth with religious rites and full military honors.

About 2,000 persons witnessed the solemn action under a bright October sun as part of the centennial celebration today.

In bursts of rhetoric, Dr. Thomas Creigh of Virginia dwelled on the meaning of that rare ritual of dust to dust again with a new touch of glory.

Those assembled here, he said, were following the lofty instincts of their nature "to gather the bones of their ancestors, place them in a metallic coffin, and cast the inspiration of their ever living virtue and valor..."

A high monument should be erected, he said, so that passengers on steamers "shall see it as they pass by, uncover their heads and toll from the bell a requiem to the memory..."

Forty-six of 1,100 Virginia militiamen were killed on the battleground here. Subsequent deaths from wounds raised the final toll to about 85.

WHAT HAPPENED to the survivors who literally went more than 1,000 different ways before they died sooner or later, before their bones went under the earth in near or distant places?

Because of incomplete or missing rosters, no one will ever know who all of them were or where they went during their short or long lives.

But it is known that many of them resumed their military careers with marked success in the American Revolution and that some attained high places in government. Records indicate that nine became governors of states or territories.

Lt. Isaac Shelby became the first governor of Kentucky. He was a general in the Revolutionary War and secretary of war in the cabinet of President James Monroe.

His father, Capt. Evan Shelby, served as governor of the short-lived state of Franklin. He became general of militia in Virginia.

Lt. John Sevier, known as "Nolachucky Jack," preceded Capt. Evan Shelby as governor of Franklin and later became the first governor of Tennessee.

Capt. George Matthews became governor of Georgia and the first member of Congress from that state.

Col. William Fleming was named acting governor of Virginia. The lead ball that entered his chest never was retrieved. The death of Fleming in 1795 — 21 years after he left here — was attributed to his wounds.

Maj. Thomas Posey was elevated to the post of the third territorial governor of Indiana. John Steele became governor of Mississippi. James Woods served as governor of Virginia and Thomas Burk as governor of North Carolina.

Capt. William Russell served as the first wagonmaster general in the Continental Army. Col. William Christian was killed by marauding Indians in Kentucky in 1786.

GEORGE CLENDENIN led a company of rangers from Camp Union to the mouth of Elk River in 1788. Near there he built a fort that marked the beginning of Charleston. The town was named for his father, Charles Clendenin.

Capt. John Stuart became county clerk of Greenbrier County and in later years was known as the historian of Dunmore's War.

Charles Simms, in whose arms Col. Charles Lewis died of wounds, became secretary of the Commonwealth of Virginia and mayor of Alexandria, VA.

Among outstanding officers who served with Dunmore's northern division of the army, but didn't participate in the battle here, were Col. Adam Stephen, Capt. George Rogers Clark and Maj. William Crawford.

Stephen became a general in the Continental Army. Clark opened up the Northwest Territory through a series of daring and brilliant moves against British forts, and Crawford was burned at the stake by Indians in 1782.

Simon Kenton, a 19-year-old messenger for Dunmore, became one of the country's greatest scouts. Simon Girty, an interpreter and scout, turned traitor to the American cause and fled to Canada.

The ultimate fates of three main leaders — Lord Dunmore, Col. Andrew Lewis and Shawnee Chief Cornstalk — are among the unusual twists in American history.

On April 21, 1775, two days after American Minutemen fired at British redcoats at Lexington and Concord, Mass., Dunmore showed his true colors. Under his orders, a supply of powder was removed from the public storehouse at Williamsburg, Va., to a British warship.

When matters got too hot, he and his family fled from the Governor's Palace to the British ship *Fowey*. On Nov. 7,1775, he declared the freedom of all Negroes, indentured servants and others who would bear arms for his majesty.

HIS LITTLE army, including runaway Negroes and others, was defeated Dec. 9,1775, by Virginians at Great Bridge, VA. On July 8,1776, he was driven from Gwynn's Island, off the coast of Virginia, by a grim general named Andrew Lewis.

Dunmore's departure marked the end of his stay in the colonies. He later served in the British House of Lords and was governor of the Bahamas. He died March 5, 1809, in Ramgate, England, at the age of 77.

The exit of Dunmore from the American scene was sweet triumph for Lewis, who had trouble in following his lordship's puzzling orders before and after the battle here.

Lewis was elevated to the rank of brigadier general. The Continental Congress never acted on a recommendation by George Washington in 1775 to make Lewis commander in chief of the army.

In 1777, Lewis resigned his commission, but he continued to be active in public affairs. On Sept. 25, 1781, he died on a return trip from Williamsburg to his home near Salem, VA.

CORNSTALK was a victim of tragic circumstances here at the fort Nov. 10, 1777, three years and one month after the battle.

The mighty Cornstalk, his subchief Red Hawk and another Indian, Old Vie (one eye), were held as hostages here Sept. 19, 1777, after they came to discuss the possibility of their tribe joining the British. They were later joined by Cornstalk's son, Elinipsico.

While they were here, a white man was killed near the fort, and a group of militiamen rushed to the fort to seek revenge.

Elinipsico trembled but Cornstalk comforted him, saying that the Great Spirit intended for them to die together.

When the militiamen entered the room, with their guns cocked and their faces pale with rage, Cornstalk bared his chest and declared:

"If any Big Knife has anything against me, let him now avenge himself.'

A volley was fired, and seven or eight bullets passed through his body. The Cornstalk fell dead.

His son was killed as he sat on a stool. Red Hawk tried to go up the chimney, but was shot down. Old Vie was badly mangled and long in the agonies of death.

THE DEATH of Cornstalk seemingly left a profound silence in the forest. The stillness deepened with the death of Mingo Chief Logan, the great orator.

Logan died in 1781, reportedly as the result of a blow from a tomahawk, wielded from behind by an unknown assailant.

Who is here today to mourn for Logan? Not one.

Celebration Marks Battle Anniversary

POINT PLEASANT

A gun roared on the old fort site here at daybreak Oct. 10, 1901. Sounds of church bells, steamboat and mill whistles followed.

The sudden and sustained bursts of sound marked the beginning of a special daylong celebration on the 127th anniversary of the Battle of Point Pleasant.

The main event was dedication of the new Tu-Endie-Wei Park, Shawnee name for the "point between two waters."

PARK BOOSTERS had come a long way since a Charleston newspaperman looked over a fence here in the spring of 1874 and got this impression of the area, then called a reservation:

"On two sides the reservation is bounded by a vegetable garden. On the third a stable with its back door next and opening into the lot. The Kanawha River bank completes the boundary."

There were later complaints about the disgrace and dishonor of stables and hog pens located near the common gravesite of the men killed in battle here.

An estimated 10,000 persons came to the 1901 event. They came in trains, boats, buggies, and wagons, on horseback and on foot. About 10 coaches, with standing room only, rolled in from Charleston on the Kanawha and Michigan railroad.

"Never before did the old town wear such a gala dress,"

a newspaper said. "Old Glory and buntings galore waved from every residence and business house."

One of the principal speakers was Mrs. Livia Nye Simpson Poffenbarger, owner and manager of the *State Gazette* at Point Pleasant and regent of the newly-formed Col. Charles Lewis Chapter of the Daughters of the American Revolution.

MRS. POFFENBARGER was a tireless and dedicated crusader for the proposition that the battle fought here Oct. 10, 1774, was the opening engagement of the American Revolution. Traditional historians then and now said that the first battle was at Lexington and Concord, Mass., April 19, 1775, or more than six months later.

In her address Mrs. Poffenbarger said several reputable historians, including President Theodore Roosevelt, had asserted that the battle here was the first in the revolution.

Broadly speaking, 1901 was a banner year for Mrs. Poffenbarger in her crusade. The park was dedicated and the DAR chapter was established.

THE CHAPTER was organized in response to her call for membership and with the understanding that its main purpose would be to raise money to construct a monument to the "first battle of the revolution."

Mrs. Poffenbarger scored heavily on May 30. 1908, with final passage of a congressional act that appropriated $10,000 to aid in erecting a monument "to commemorate the battle of the revolution."

The crusaders were recognized as the moving force behind the act. What pleased her was the language in the act, which she wanted more than the money.

Thus, in 1908, Congress went on record as stating that the Battle of Point Pleasant was a "battle of the revolution."

This point of law remains the general theme today in the position taken by Patricia Burton, lecturer and writer under the incorporated name of America's Frontier Ltd. She is regarded today as one of the main torchbearers of the "Point Pleasant first" concept.

Miss Burton, a consultant in history for the Mason County Bicentennial Commission, doesn't pretend to be a historian in the traditional sense. As a trained and experienced abstracter, she simply cites official records in support of her views.

However, she has done about 10 years of independent research on Dunmore's War. On the basis of that research, she has a strong opinion that Dunmore's agent, Maj. John Connolly, was the real villain behind the whole Point Pleasant affair.

Mrs. Poffenbarger, after passage of the 1908 legislation, continued her Point Pleasant first crusade for many years.

She was at the center of the stage Oct. 9. 1909, when about 25,000 persons came here to celebrate what the Point Pleasant Register called the "proudest day in West Virginia.'

The main event was the unveiling of the new monument — an 84-foot granite shaft in the middle of the two-acre park, with an eight-foot statue of a colonial soldicr facing east at the base.

Gov. William E. Glasscock and his staff rode on horseback in the parade. Following in carriages were members of West Virginia's congressional delegation, including Sen. Nathan B. Scott, Rep. W. P. Hubbard and Rep. James A. Hughes.

A decorated wagon carried 13 little boys, who helped in the unveiling exercise. One of them was 3-year-old Charles Cameron Lewis, Great-great-great grandson of Col. Charles Lewis, who was killed in the battle here.

Mrs. Poffenbarger was praised repeatedly by speakers during an afternoon program and banquet session. State Auditor J. S. Darst told the assembled citizens:

"Without your Mrs. Livia Simpson Poffenbarger you would have no monument today to unveil. She built your monument."

MRS. POFFENBARGER published a book in 1909, entitled

Battle of Point Pleasant: First Battle of the American Revolution, Oct. 10, 1774. In the book she quoted this sweeping statement from Theodore Roosevelt's book, *Winning of the West*:

"Lord Dunmore's War, waged by Americans for the good of America, was the opening act in the drama whereof the closing scene was played at Yorktown."

However, in the same book, Roosevelt rejected the contention that Dunmore betrayed the Virginians during Dunmore's War. In a footnote, Roosevelt said of Dunmore:

"There is no reason whatever to suppose that he was not doing his best for the Virginians: he deserved their gratitude, and he got it for the time being."

Mrs. Poffenbarger made it clear that her case rested mainly on the theory that Dunmore was involved in a plot to destroy the Virginia militia at Point Pleasant through an alliance with the Indians.

"We. . . give these many details of evidence that the Battle of Point Pleasant, while not a battle between the English and colonial forces, nevertheless shed the first blood on American soil for American independence," she writes.

"It can be plainly seen that, though at this time these sturdy pioneers were fighting to protect their homes and firesides, the very foundation of national government, Great Britain, through her Tory governor of Virginia, intended thus to destroy the flower of the colonial army of Virginia."

In the early 1930s, the Point Pleasant Battle Commission, with Mrs. Poffenbarger as president, published a pamphlet in which she resumed arguments in favor of the first battle concept and enlarged upon them.

In support of her views, Mrs. Poffenbarger quoted from the works of John Stuart, a participant in the battle; Alexander Scott Withers, whose *Chronicles of Border Warfare* was first published in 1831; Samuel Kercheval, *History of the Valley of Virginia*, first published in 1833, and John P. Hale, *Trans-Allegheny Pioneers*, 1886, among others. One of the strongest statements was made by O. E. Randall, listed as an eminent historian in Ohio:

> *"View as you choose, the Dunmore War was the preclude, the opening occasion of the American Revolution."*

Was the first battle fought here?

CHAPTER 17

PEACEFUL POINT BELIES BATTLE

POINT PLEASANT, W. Va., October, 1974

"The same great rivers meet and mingle here
"That on that day of doubt and dread and fear
"Flowed calmly on, unheedful of the strife,
"The sound of battle and the wreck of life.
"Now sweet the sunlight falls upon the dell.
"Where heroes fought and brave Charles Lewis fell."

So wrote Harry Maxwell Smythe as a centennial ode.

So it is on the occasion of the bicentennial observance.

On the point, in beautiful Tu-Endie-Wei Park, it's difficult to realize that a great and terrible battle was fought here 200 years ago.

A towering battle monument serves as a permanent reminder. Near it is the common grave of the 46 and more Virginia militiamen who died here. A single stone for one man, Charles Lewis (1736-1774), is in the center of the grave.

All of Virginia was saddened by the death of the popular Lewis in the battle here on Oct. 10, 1774. He was the ranking officer killed and the brother of the commanding officer, Col. Andrew Lewis.

Col. Charles Lewis' wife, mother of seven children, descended to the very depths of despair when news of the death reached the family home on Cowpasture River in what is now Bath County, VA. She also lost a brother and half-brother in the battle.

Her seventh child was born Sept. 11, 1774, a month before the battle. The fallen colonel never saw his son.

BY REASON of that birth, another Charles Lewis lives today. The great-great-great grandson of the colonel lives within approximately two miles of the battlefield.

Today's Charles Lewis, 68, lives on a 1,234-acre Ohio River farm in a sprawling white brick mansion built in 1866.

He is a modest, pleasant man with blue eyes and light, graying hair. Physically fit, he chins himself daily, stands 5 feet, 10 inches tall, and weighs 150 pounds.

A lifetime farmer with an interest in business and cultural affairs, he is a graduate of West Virginia University School of Agriculture.

The modern Lewis, five generations down from the colonel, is unmarried. "The buck stops here," he says with a smile.

A sister with the revered family name of Margaret Lynn Lewis (same as the mother of the colonel) and a brother, William Lewis, also live at the family home here. Both are unmarried.

However, the bloodline continues through two other sisters, Mrs. Virginia Harper of Buffalo, N.Y., who has a son and three grandchildren: and Mrs. Annette Seidel, Jr., wife of the first secretary of the American embassy in Beirut, Lebanon, who has two sons and a daughter.

The farm has the corporate name of Old Town Farm, Inc. The Indians crossed it on their way to the Battle of Point Pleasant.

When the original colonel was mortally wounded, he carried a heavy pocket watch with a thick crystal in a silvery case. On the inside of the case were bits of decorative paper in the shape of an arrow through a heart.

The watch, made in London and stored in the vault of a Point Pleasant bank, is one of Charles Lewis' proud possessions today. He also has a lieutenant's original commission granted to that seventh child on May 1, 1794, and signed by President George Washington.

The 19-year-old lieutenant fought with Mad Anthony Wayne in his big victory over Indians in the Battle of Fallen Timbers, 1794.

Lewis has another proud possession. It is the private memoirs of the life of his father, who died in his 90th year in 1964.

Written in a casual style, with a literary talent and a sense of humor shining through, the autobiography notes that Lewis family members were French Huguenots, who immigrated to Scotland in 1598 and later to Ireland.

Patriarch John Lewis and family emigrated to America after he killed an Irish landlord in retaliation for the killing of his brother.

INCIDENTALLY, the father of today's Charles Lewis wrote:

"Cornstalk was a great man. An analysis of the campaign shows that he outgeneraled the whites."

In his memoirs the father added that Lord Dunmore used bad strategy in remaining far removed from the commander of the southern division, Col. Andrew Lewis. He said Andrew Lewis erred in failing to build a fort or post an advance guard to prevent an attack.

The memoirs essentially denied reports that the original Charles was wearing a scarlet uniform when he fell, but conceded that he wore a red vest.

The five men who preceded the present Lewis are buried practically within an arrow's flight of each other — the colonel at Tu-Endie-Wei, two in the family cemetery and two in the community cemetery.

Four of the five were named Charles Lewis. The exception was Peter Steenbergen Lewis, grandfather of the Charles of today.

The family has lived on the farm here since the second Charles, the sub-lieutenant, came from Greenbrier County. According to tradition, his arrival was on Oct. 10, 1800, the 26th anniversary date of the battle.

In addition to the Lewis family of today, it's believed there are many thousands of direct descendants of participants in the battle here.

Harry B. Lambert, a Charleston lawyer, descends from 16-year-old James B. Lambert, who applied for his pension at the age of 86 in Ripley County, Indiana. His affidavit stated that he campaigned against Indians under Col. Andrew Lewis and "this applicant received several balls through the clothes" on the day of the battle.

The descendants of Joshua Morris, one of six brothers said to have participated in the battle, include Judge James Lee Thompson of the 29th circuit; former Kanawha Intermediate Judge William J. Thompson of St. Albans, Mrs. E. Forrest Jones and Mrs. Donald Carnohan of Huntington. Joshua was a son of William Morris Sr., whose family members were the first permanent white settlers in the Kanawha Valley at a spot now called Cedar Grove.

AMONG other descendants is Jack Burdett, Point Pleasant lawyer and coordinator of the Mason County Bicentennial Commission. As a boy he played around the base of the battle monument and sometimes swam the Ohio River when his mother wasn't looking. He is descended from a soldier named James Hill.

In preparation for the centennial celebration, he thoroughly reviewed the history of the battle. He established positions and computed distances to reconstruct the conflict in relation to city streets.

He knows that the battle line stabilized approximately at Sixth Street and that the first shot was fired in the vicinity of Central Elementary School at 12th and Main streets.

He has accumulated much information about forts and bones.

Three forts have stood on the battleground: small Fort Blair, erected within a month after the battle; larger Fort Randolph, built in 1776 and burned by Indians in 1779; and a second Fort Randolph built in 1785.

The fort constructed for the bicentennial service is a replica of the first Fort Randolph. Included in this $99,000 structure are pine stockade logs from Montgomery, Ala., cabin materials from Fletcher, N. C., and cedar shakes from Orrville, Ohio.

The history of bones begins with reburial of some of the remains of Virginians for ceremonial purposes in the centennial celebration of 1874.

About 1890 some more bones were found during the building of a road through a section of the battleground.

Not generally known is the fact that 30 to 40 skeletons of Indians were found on a hill above the battleground at about the same time in 1890.

The first skeleton was found by a laborer in search of rocks for a rock garden. He thought he had found the body of someone murdered and rushed into town with the news.

AN INVESTIGATION revealed a veritable landslide of skeletons in tiers, with evidence that they were covered by tree branches and blankets as well as the earth. Further checking by experts showed that the skeletons were well over 100 years old and that they probably were uncounted victims in the battle.

It was theorized that the Indians carried many of their dead to the burial spot on the hill the night after the battle while Virginians were asleep or sitting around campfires or taking care of their wounded.

Some of the skulls of the Indians were varnished and kept in a local doctor's office for several years.

The burial site of Chief Cornstalk, murdered here in 1777, remained a mystery for a long period. About 1832 an old man walked into town and told interested persons they could find Cornstalk's remains by digging down four feet at Second and Viand streets. He was right.

The remains were reburied in the courthouse lawn, and then buried a third time in Tu-Endie-Wei Park in 1954. A monument marks the grave.

During this bicentennial observance, it is natural to move around town, looking for connections between the long past, the present and future.

In that perspective, two rows of double-headed parking meters have to be among the most unusual sights in town.

Standing like metallic, futuristic soldiers, they face each other at one end of Sixth Street, the stabilized battle line. They are jammed up close to the floodwall, site of the old Silver Bridge abutment, now sealed off.

Photograph by Rod Brand

FORTY-SIX persons died when the Silver Bridge fell Dec. 15, 1967. Forty-six men in the Virginia army fell dead on the day of the battle, although the count later increased to an estimated 75 as wounded men died.

It's all just coincidental, but the relationship is haunting. What does the future hold in relation to the past?

One can look at the mingling waters of two great rivers and hope they have tingling secrets to tell.

But the rivers just keep rolling along, by the place where heroes fought and brave Charles Lewis fell.

AND IN 1974— RECONSTRUCTED FORT DEDICATED

The Mason County Bicentennial Commission sponsored an eight-day celebration in observance of the Battle of Point Pleasant. This story covers the events on Oct. 10, 1974, highlight of the observance and the 200th anniversary date of the battle.

POINT PLEASANT

This growing river city is the "birthplace of the nation," Governor Arch Moore declared here Thursday, the 200th anniversary of the Battle of Point Pleasant.

"The battle waged here triggered the drama of gaining our national independence of the British crown."

The Governor was the principal speaker at the dedication of reconstructed Ft. Randolph. About 700 persons attended this main event in an eight-day bicentennial observance.

Looking into a bright mid-afternoon sun and speaking from a stage within the stockade area of the fort, Moore continued:

"We are dedicating today more than just a structure commemorating an event of our nation's birth. This fort should be a reminder to all our citizens that in order for our nation to remain great and strong we must reaffirm our strength and potential as a free people. Just as the American Revolution was a beginning, so is this observance and the bicentennial a beginning."

Thus the Governor all but said that the first battle of the American Revolution was fought here. Traditional historians say the first battle was fought six months later at Lexington and Concord in Massachusetts.

IN ANY EVENT, the ceremony here Thursday officially launched the bicentennial celebration in West Virginia. Point Pleasant is one of five key sites that have special import for the observance. The others are Berkeley Springs, location of the first summer White House, the custom house at Wheeling, the Mother's Day shrine in Grafton and Blennerhassett Island at Parkersburg.

Moore formally presented cheeks totaling $34,500 to officials here for the Bicentennial Drama Inc. "Rivers of Destiny," an outdoor musical drama based on events related to the battle, was shown to a full house here Thursday night. There will be additional showings at 7:30 p.m. today, Saturday and Sunday. Other bicentennial events will be held during the three days here.

The Governor was escorted into the fort by Michael Shaw, member of the House of Delegates from Mason County, Point Pleasant Mayor John Musgrave and seven men dressed in the homespun garb of Virginia militiamen.

The Point Pleasant High School Band provided incidental music for Thursday's occasion. Majorettes performed during a bicentennial march.

Many descendants of those who fought in the battle attended the ceremony Thursday. They identified themselves by wearing red shawls.

Among them were William and Margaret Lynn Lewis, both direct descendants of Col. Charles Lewis and both residents on a farm near here.

LEON GLASSBURN, of California, descendant of a Virginia militiaman with the same last name, is believed to have traveled farthest to attend the ceremony.

Perry Poffenbarger, a Charleston lawyer and son of the late Mrs. Livia Nye Simpson Poffenbarger, was formally recognized. The son is a direct descendant of a militiaman. Mrs. Poffenbarger crusaded for erection of the battle monument and for designation of the battle as the first in the American Revolution.

Jack Burdett, descendant of a militiaman named James Hill, served as master of ceremonies. He wore a coonskin cap and a complete buckskin outfit.

Sen. Robert Griffin of Michigan, the Minority Whip in the Senate, arranged for the reading in cooperation with West Virginia senators Robert C. Byrd and Jennings Randolph.

This unusual tribute was given at the request of Patricia Burton of Troy, Mich., a historical consultant on the bicentennial observance and a technical expert on Dunmore's War.

Mayor and Mrs. John G. Hutchinson of Charleston were among guests here. Also recognized were Everett Lutton, contractor for construction of the fort; and Jack C. Meenach, who designed it. The cost was about $99,000.

THE ORIGINAL fort, erected in 1776, served as a key outpost for about three years. It was burned by Indians in 1779. A second Fort Randolph was built in 1785.

The weather Thursday was similar to that on Oct. 10 two centuries ago, although perhaps a bit warmer. The real battle started at sunup and ended at sundown. About 1,100 Virginians under Col. Andrew Lewis defeated an estimated 1,000 Indians under Chief Cornstalk in the historic conflict.

At the end of Thursday's event, a mock defense of the fort was conducted by members of the Mountaineer Flintlock Rifle Club under the command of their president, Robert Walden.

The men climbed high in a sheltered corner of the stockade and fired bursts of black powder through large loopholes. The men yelled robustly during the peals of musketry. One wounded fellow slid down the stairs.

When the shooting and yelling subsided, Burdett declared it was safe for everyone to go home.

CHAPTER 19

ACKNOWLEDGMENTS

This series of newspaper stories was literally made possible by the library of the West Virginia Department of Achieves and History, along with the endless patience and ready assistance of the entire library staff and the acting department director, Mrs. Pearl Rogers.

The Roy Bird Cook Room of the Kanawha County Public Library, with generous additional staff assistance, was an oasis of materials in a vast desert of knowledge about what happened at Point Pleasant in 1774.

The lectures and writings of Patricia Burton, a technical expert on Dunmore's War, provided rich details, helpful guideposts and information unobtainable elsewhere.

Jack Burdett, coordinator of the Mason County Bicentennial Commission, was a model of cooperation in the sharing of background information and on-site knowledge of the battlefield.

Dr. Elizabeth Comets shared her general wisdom of history with appropriate perspective and gave valuable advice.

Kenneth R. MacDonald, Jr., a doctoral candidate at West Virginia University, loaned a scholarly manuscript.

Charles C. Lewis gave of his time and very special knowledge, and provided access to his father's memoirs. Mr. Lewis is the great-great-great grandson of the ranking officer killed in the battle, Col. Charles Lewis.

Special letters, which helped profoundly to make a decision on a point of history, were written by Dr. Howard Peckham, Robert H. Land, George Parkinson and Dr. Otis K. Rice.

Many other persons were helpful in various ways. Among them were:

Mayor John Musgrave of Point Pleasant, Charles Lanham, president of the Mason County Bicentennial Commission; Mrs. Eldridge Sauer, regent of the Col Charles Lewis Chapter, Daughters of the American Revolution; Mrs. E. Forrest Jones, S. Louise Bing, Perry Poffenbarger, Forest J. Bowman, Harry Lambert, Harold Lambert, Mr. and Mrs. Kenneth D. Swope, and C. Robert Leith.

A deep debt of gratitude to all persons mentioned or possibly forgotten is hereby acknowledged.

— *J.G.M.*

Basic materials used in writing this series of newspaper stories are from the Lyman C. Draper Manuscript Collection, with special references to sections entitled Border Forays, Preston Papers and Virginia Papers. The collection, owned by the State Historical Society of Wisconsin, is on microfilm in the West Virginia Department of Archives and History Library.

Fundamental use also was made of *Documentary History of Dunmore's War*, by Reuben Gold Thwaites and Louise Phelps Kellogg, Madison, Wis., 1905; and *History of the Battle of Point Pleasant*, by Virgil A. Lewis, Charleston, 1909.

Other main sources:

Abernethy, Thomas P., *Western Lands and the American Revolution*, New York, 1937.

American Archives, fourth series, contemporary documents and reports in the colonial period, Washington, 1839.

Caley, Percy J., Dunmore, *Colonial Governor of New York and Virginia, 1770-1782*, unpublished doctoral dissertation, University of Pittsburgh, 1939.

Caruso, John Anthony, *The Appalachian Frontier: America's First Surge Westward*, Indianapolis, MD, 1959.

Dayton, Ruth Woods, *Greenbrier Pl oneers and Their Homes*, Charleston, 1942.

de Gruyter, Julius A., *The Kanawha Spectator*, Charleston, 1953.

Doddridge, Dr. Joseph, *Logan, the Last of the Race of Shikellemus Chief of the Cayuga Nation*, a reprint, Parsons, W. Va., 1971.

Downes, Randolph C., *Council Fires on the Upper Ohio*, Pittsburgh, 1940.

Eckert, Allan W., *The Frontiersmen*, Boston, 1967.

Other Sources:

Hale, John P., *History of the Great Kanawha Valley*, two volumes, Madison, Wis., 1891.

Hale, John P., *Trans-Allegheny Pioneers: Historical Sketches of the First White Settlers West of the Alleghenies*, Cincinnati, 1886.

Hale, John P., and others in *History of the Upper Ohio Valley*, Madison, Wis., 1891.

Jacob, John Jeremiah, *A Biographical Sketch of the Life of the Late Captain Michael Cresap*, a reprint, Parsons, W. Va., 1971.

MacDonald, Kenneth R. Jr., *The Battle of Point Pleasant and the American Revolution*, unpublished doctoral dissertation, West Virginia University, 1974.

Poffenbarger, Mrs. Livia Nye Simpson, *The Battle of Point Pleasant, A Battle of the Revolution*, Point Pleasant, 1909.

Randall, E.O. and D. Ryan, *History of Ohio*, New York, 1912.

Rice. Otis K., *The Allegheny Frontier: West Virginia Beginnings, 1730-1830.*

Roosevelt Theodore, *Winning of the West*, a modern abridgment, New York, 1963.

Stuart, John, *Memorial of Indian Wars and Other Occurrences By the Late Col. Stuart of Green Brier*, Parsons, W. Va., 1971.

Withers, Alexander Scott, *Chronicles of Border Warfare*, Cincinnati, 1903.

Magazines:

Burton, Patricia, "Point Pleasant — 197 Years Later," *Wonderful West Virginia*, December, 1971; January, February, 1972.

Downes, Randolph C., "Dunmore's War: An Interpretation," *Mississippi Valley Historical Review*, XXI (December, 1934), 311-19.

Hunter, William H., "First Battle of the American Revolution," *Ohio Archaeological and Historical Quarterly*, XI, 1903; 93-102.

Largent, Robert J., "Lord Dunmore's War," *West Virginia Review*, three articles, 1937.

Mahon, John K., "Anglo-American Methods of. Indian Warfare, 1676-1794," *Mississippi Valley Historical Review*, XLV (September, 1958), 258-272.

Malone, Eva Grant, "Sketch of Andrew Lewis and Battle of Point Pleasant," *West Virginia Historical Magazine Quarterly*, (April, 1904), 94-108.

Randall, E.O., "The Dunmore War," *West Virginia Historical Magazine Quarterly*, ill (January, 1903), 23-44.

Sosin, Jack M., "The British Indian Department and Lord Dunmore's War," *Virginia Magazine of History and Biography*, v.74, 1966; 34-50.

Wrick, Elizabeth, "Dunmore — Virginia's Last Royal Governor," *West Virginia History, A Quarterly Magazine*, VIII, (1947), 237-282.

Public Records and Reports:

"Battle of Point Pleasant, First Bottle of the American Revolution," a compilation of reports and federal and state legislative acts by the Point Pleasant Battle Monument Commission, about 1936.

Executive Journals, Council of Colonial Virginia, 1754-1775, v. 6.

First Continental Congress records, Sept. 5-Oct. 26, 1774.

Virginia House of Burgesses Journal, 1774. West Virginia Auditor's Office, Land Department, copies of original land grants, listed in "Sims' Index to Land Grants in West Virginia."

APPENDIX I

Known Participants In the First Battle of the American Revolution

Alphabetical list of the names, yet preserved, of the men who participated in the Battle of Point Pleasant, First Battle of the American Revolution, October 10, 1774.

The Virginia colonial troops were commanded by Colonel Andrew Lewis, later Brigadier General Andrew Lewis, of Virginia.

Virgil A. Lewis, State Historian and Archivist, writing of the national character of the Battle of Point Pleasant, has said:

"It is the greatest event in the Colonial Period and stands just at its close—with it, the Revolution begins. It is the connecting link between the two greatest periods in all American history—closing as it does the one, and opening the other."

Mr. Lewis further says of the men of the Battle:

"Six of them afterwards occupied seats in the American House of Representatives; three were members of the United States Senate; four of them became Governors of States; one of them a territorial Governor; one of them a Military and Civil Commandant of Upper Louisiana. Seven officers in this Battle of Point Pleasant rose to the rank of General. Six captains of that Battle commanded regiments on Continental Establishments in the War for Independence. Four officers of that Battle led the attack of Gwynn's Island, July 1776, that dislodged Dunmore, the Tory Governor of Virginia, and drove him forever from the shores of Virginia.

"Hundreds of the men of the Battle participated on Revolutionary battlefields and one follow, age 63 years, at the Battle of the Thames in 1813, secured a victory that broke the British power in the Northwest. Many of the men of Point Pleasant Battle witnessed the surrender of Cornwallis at Yorktown."

(See Page 35, Vol. II, West Virginia Historical Magazine. April, 1903.)

AUTHORIZED ROSTER

No Official Roster having ever been prepared, the following Concurrent Resolution No. 17 was adopted by the Legislature of West Virginia of March 1,1935, as follows:

"That the Point Pleasant Battle Monument Commission be and is hereby authorized and requested to cause to be inscribed on bronze tablets to be attached to the base of the Point Pleasant Battle Monument, when such base shall have been provided for the names of all the officers and men who participated in the battle of the Revolution fought on October tenth, one thousand seven hundred and seventy-four, at Point Pleasant, now West Virginia, as ascertained and listed by the Point Pleasant Battle Monument Commission, under the provisions of Chapter forty-three, Acts of the Legislature of West Virginia, one thousand nine hundred and thirty-one and reported to the Governor, and to provide space on such tables for inscription of the names of such other officers and men who participated in said battle as shall hereafter be ascertained and listed under the provisions of said chapter forty-three for that session of the Legislature."

A

Able, Jeremiah
Adams, John
Adkins, Milton
Adkins, Parker
Agnew, (Agnue) John
Alden, Andrew
Alexander, James, Sr.
Allen, Hugh, Lieut.
Allen, James
Allen, Thomas
Alley, Thomas
Alliet, (Elliot) Robt.
Alsbury, Thomas
Anderson, James
Anderson, Samuel
Andrews, Samuel
Arbuckle, John
Arbuckle, Matthew, Capt.
Arbuckle, William
Ard, James
Armstrong, George
Armstrong, Thomas
Armstrong, William
Arnold, James
Arnold, Steven
Arthur, John
Astle, Samuel
Atkins, Blackburn
Atkins, Charles
Atkins, Henry
Atkins, William

B

Babbitt, Ishmel
Bailey, Campbell
Bailey, James
Bailey, John
Baker, Markham
Baker, Martin
Baker, Samuel, Ensign
Ball, James
Bambridge, James
Barnes,—
Barker, Thomas
Baret, Edward
Barton, Samuel
Bazel, John
Barkley, John
Barnett, James
Barnett, S. L.
Bates,—
Batson, Mordica
Baugh, Jacob
Baylston, Wm.
Bateman, Abraham Moore
Bateman, Charles Davis
Bateman, Daniel Omnsbury
Bell, James
Bell, Thomas
Bellow, Daniel (canoe man)
Bergman, Christian
Berry, Francis
Bishop, Levi
Blackburn, Arthur
Blackford, Joseph
Blair, Daniel
Blair, Francis
Blair, William
Blankenship, Richard
Bledsoe, Abraham, Lieut.
Blesley, Jacob
Blesley, John
Boles, John
Boh, Adam
Boh, Jacob
Bojard, Abraham
Boniface, Wm.
Bonnifield, Samuel
Borg, Francis
Boughman, Jacob
Boughman, John
Burney, Thomas
Bowen, Reese
Bowen, William
Bowles, Sergt.
Bowles, Robert
Bowyer, Henry
Boyd, James
Boyd, Robert
Boyer, Henry
Boyles, Barney
Boylston,
Bracken, Matthew (Ensign and Lieut.)
Bradley, John
Boughman, John
Bowen, Moses
Brombridge, James
Broomstead, Andrew
Bradley, Wm.
Bramstead, Andrew
Breckenridge, Alexander (Captain)
Breden, John
Breeze, Robert
Breeze, Richard
Brooks, George
Brooks, Charles
Brown, James
Brown, Low
Brown, Moses
Brown, Robert
Brown. Thomas
Brown, William
Brumfield, Humphrey
Brumfield, Solomon
Brumley, Thomas
Brundge, Solomon
Bryans, Shorgan
Bryans, Wm., Sergt.
Bryant, Wm.
Buch, John, Sergt.
Buch, William
Buckhannan, Commissariat
Buchnall, John
Buchanan, John. Col.
Buchanan, Wm., Ensign
Buford, Abraham, Col.
Bunch, Jasper
Bunch, Joseph
Buford, Thomas, Capt.
Burch, Joseph

Burch, Richard
Burcks, Samuel
Burke, Thomas
Burne, Thomas
Burney, John
Burnsides, James
Burens, James
Burroughs, John
Burton, Litton
Burchfield, James
Bush. John, Sergt.
Buster, David
Butler, Joseph
Butler, Shadrick
Buster, Wallace
Buster, William
Butterford, Ben
Byrd, Richard
Byrne, Charles

C

Calloway, Dudley
Cameron, George
Cameron, Hugh
Campbell, Arthur
Campbell, John, Capt.
Campbell, Joseph
Campbell, Robert
Campbell, Samuel
Campbell, Wm., Capt.
Canaday, Thos.
Caperton, Adam
Caperton, Hugh
Carlton, James
Carmack, John
Carney, Martin
Carpenter, John
Carpenter, Jeremiah
Carpenter, Solomon
Carpenter, Thomas
Carr, George
Carr, James
Carr, John
Carr, William
Catrain, James
Cartoon, Joel
Cartoon, John
Carter, John
Carther, Edward
Cary, Jeremiah
Casey, Wm.
Cashady, Simon
Cashed, Thomas
Carton, Adam
Carton, Francis
Carton, Jacob
Carton, Michael
Catron, Peter
Catron, Philip
Cats, Rodger
Cattes, John
Cavenaugh, Charles
Cavenaugh, Philemon
Cavenaugh, Philip
Cavenaugh, Wm.
Cecil, Benj. Sollers
Champ, Wm.
Chapline, Abraham
Chapman, John
Chapman, Richard
Charlton, Tames
Chesney, John
Christian, Wm. Col.
Clark, John
Clark, James
Clark, Samuel
Clay, David
Clay, Mitchell
Clay, Zekel
Clendinen, Adam
Clendinen, Alexander
Clendinen, Charles
Clendinen, Geo., Capt.
Clendinen, Robert
Clendinen, Wm., Capt.
Clerk. John
Coils, James
Clifton, Wm.
Clinding, George
Clinding, Wm.
Cloyne, Nicholas
Coile, James
Coiler, John
Coiler, Mease, Sergt.
Collet, Thos.
Cochran, Wm.
Collens, Richard
Cocke, William, Capt.
Condon, David (canoe man)
Canner, Patrick
Conner, William
Constantine, Patrick
Cook, David
Cook, Henry
Cook, John
Cook, William
Cooper, Abraham
Cooper, Francis
Cooper, Leonard, Lieut.
Cooper, Nathaniel
Cooper, Spencer
Cooper, Thomas
Copley, Thomas
Corder, John
Cormick, John
Cornwell, Adam
Cornwell, John
Courtney, Charles
Courtney, John
Cowen, John
Cowen, Jared
Coward, —
Cox, Gabriel, Lieut.
Cox, John, Capt.
Coyle, James
Crabtree, Wm. (Scout)
Craigh, George
Craig, John
Craigh, Wm., Sergt.
Cram, John
Cram, Joseph, Sergt.
Craven, Joseph
Craven, James
Craven, John

Craven, Robert
Crockett, Walter, Capt.
Crawford, Alexander
Crawford, Bonard
Crawford, John, Sergt.
Crawley, (Croley) James
Creed, Matthew
Crisman, Isaac
Crockett, Joseph
Croley, Samuel
Crow, John, Sergt.
Crow, Wm.
Curwill, Alexander
Cundiff, Jonathan Ensign
Cunningham, James
Cunningham, John
Curry, James
Cutlip, David
Cutright, John
Culwell, Alexander

D

Dale, James
Davis, Azriah, Capt.
Davis, Charles
Davis, George
Davis, Robert (Scout)
Davis, Samuel
Davies, Jonathan
Day, Joseph
Day, William
Deal, Wm.
Deek, John
Demonse, Abraham
Deniston, John
Denton, John
Dickinson, John, Col.
Dillon, Lieut.
Dingos, Peter
Diver, John
Doack, David
Doack, John
Doack, Robt., Capt.
Doack, Samuel
Doack, Wm., Ensign
Dobler, Jacob
Dodd, John
Dodd, James
Dorherty, John
Dorherty, James
Dollarhide, Samuel
Donaley, James, Sergt.
Donaley, John, (fifer)
Donaldson, John, Capt.
Donalson, Robert
Donalson, Thomas
Dooley, Jacob
Dooley, Thomas, Lieut.
Doran, Patrick
Doss, Joel
Dougherty, Geo., Sergt.
Dougherty, James
Dougherty, John
Dougherty, Michael, Sergt.
Douglas, George
Douglas, James
Downy, James, Sergt.
Douny, John
Drake, Ephriam
Drake, Joseph
Draper, John, Lieut.
Dunaho, James
Dulin, James
Dunkirk, John, Sergt.
Dunlap, Robert
Dunaho, John
Dutton, John
Dutton, Philip
Dyer, Wm.

E

Eager, John
Eastham, George
Eastham, William
Edgar, Thomas
Edmunston, (Edmondson) Wm., Lieut.
Edwards, James
Edwards, Jonathan
Egins, Edward
Elkins, Jesse
Ellenborough, Peter
Elias, Thomas
Elliott, Robert, Capt.
Ellison, Charles
Ellison, James
Elswick, John
English, Joseph
English, Joshua
English, Stephen
Ensminger, John
Estill, Samuel
Evans, Andrew
Evans, Eran
Ewing, Alexander
Ewing, Alexander, Jr.
Ewing, Robert
Ewing, Samuel
Ewing, Samuel, Sergt.-Major
Ewing, William

F

Fain, John
Fain, Samuel
Fargison, Thomas
Farley, John
Farley, (Farlon) Thos.
Farmer, Nathan
Feavil, Wm.,
Ferrill, Robt.
Ferrill, Wm.
Field, John, Col.
Fielde, Wm.
Fielde, John, Sergt.
Finquay, Isham (canoe man)
Fielder, Wm.
Findley, George
Findley, John
Findley, Robt., Sergt.
Fisher, Isaac
Fitzhugh, John
Fitzpatrick, Timothy

Fleming, Wm., Col.
Flintham, John
Fliping, Thos.
Floyd, John
Fourgeson, Thomas
Fowler, James (Scout)
Fowler, Samuel
Fowler, William
Franklin, James
Franklin, Wm.
Frazer, John
Freeland, John
Friel, Jeremiah
Frogg, John, Lieut.
Fry, George
Fry, George, Jr.
Fry, John
Fullen, Daniel
Fullen, James
Fuls, George

G

Gardner, Andrew
Garrett, William
Gass, David (Messenger)
Gatliff (Gallepp), Sq.
Gibbs, Luman, (Scout)
Gibson, George, Lieut.
Gibson, Joseph
Gilbert, Thomas
Gillihan (Gilliland), John
Gilkenson, James
Gill, Prisley
Gilespy, Thomas
Gillass, Wm.
Gillian, Duncan
Gilmore, James, Capt.
Gilmore, John
Givens, John, Lieut.-Capt.
Gloscum, David
Glass, Wm.
Glaves, Michael
Glenn, Davis
Goff, Andrew
Goldman, Edw., Lieut.
Goaldsby,
Goodall, John
Gordon, Moses
Gormon, David
Graham, Benj.
Green, John
Greer, John
Griffin, Robert
Griger, Peter
Grigsby, John
Grim, John
Gribsby,
Guffy, James
Guillen, Edward
Guillon, Barney
Gurden, Michael
Guillen, Duncan

H

Hackett, Thomas
Hackworth, Augustine
Hackworth, Wm.
Hagel,—
Haines, Lewis
Hale, Edward
Hale, Thomas
Hale, William
Hall, Francis
Hall, James
Hall, Thomas
Hamilton, Francis
Hamilton, Isaiah
Hamilton, Jacob
Hamilton, James
Hamilton, John
Hamilton, Thomas
Hammond, Philip
Hamrick, Thomas
Hamrick, Wm.
Handley (Herrill), Robert
Handley (Hensley), Samuel
Hanee, Philip
Hannan, Thomas
Hansburger, Adam
Hanson, Wm.
Harlon, Elijah
Harlan, Silas
Harmon, Dangerfield
Harmon, George
Harmon, Israel
Harmon, John
Harrel, Wm. (Scout)
Harriman, Sked, Sergt.
Harris, Griffon
Harris, John
Harris, Stephen
Harrison, Andrew
Harrison, Benj., Capt.
Harrison, John Lieut.
Harrod, James, Capt.
Hart, Thomas
Hasket, Thos.
Hatfield, Andrew
Havens, James
Havens, John
Hayes, John
Haynes, Benj.
Haynes, Joseph, Capt.
Hays, Charles
Hays, Samuel
Henley, George
Henley, William
Hensley (Hadley), Samuel
Herbert, William, Capt.
Herd, Richard
Herrill, Robert
Henderson, Alexander
Henderson, Daniel
Henderson, John, Lieut.
Henderson, Samuel
Hendrix, Peter
Hays, Samuel (Scout)
Head, Anthony, (Messenger)
Hedden, Thomas
Hepenstahl (Hempinstall), Abraham
Hickman,—
Higgans (Higans), Peter

Higgans, Philemon
Hill, Capt.
Hill, James
Hill, Robert
Hobbs, Vincent
Hogan, Henry
Hogan, William
Holley, William
Holloway, Richard
Holston, Stephen
Holwell, Walter
Hornes, Lewis
Hooper, Wm.
Hopton, Stephen
Hopton, William
Home, Joseph
Howard, Charles
Howard, Henry
Huff, Leonard
Huff, Peter
Huff, Samuel
Huff, Thomas
Hutchinson, Lewis
Hutchinson, William
Hughes, Davy
Hughes, Jesse, (Scout)
Hughes, Ellis
Hughey, James
Hughey, Joseph
Humphries, John
Hundley, John
Hunter, Robert
Huston, John
Hynes, Francis

I

Ingles, Wm., Major
Ingles, Joshua
Ingles, Thomas
Inglish (English), Joseph
Inglish (English), Joshua
Irvin, John
Isum, Wm.

J

Jackson, Yerty
Jameson, John
Jenkins, Jeremiah
Jennings, Edmond
Jewitt, Matthew
Johns, William
Johnson, Arthur, Capt.
Johnson, John
Johnston, Patrick
Jones, Benjamin
Jones, John
Jones, Thomas

K

Kasheday, Peter
Kenneson, Charles
Keith, Samuel
Kelly, Alexander
Kelly, Garrott
Kelsey, John
Kendrics, James
Kennedy, Ezekiel
Kennedy, Thomas
Kennedy, Wm., Sergt.
Kinneson, Charles
Kinneson, Edward
Kennot, Zacariah
Kerr, James
Kerr, William
Kinder, George
Kinder, Jacob
Kinder, Peter
King, James
King, John
King, William
Kincaid (Kingheid), David, Jr.
Kincaid (Kingheid), George
Kincaid (Kingheid), James
Kincaid (Kingheid), John, Sergt.
Kinnison, Michael
Kinnison, Walter
Kishnor, Andrew, Sr.
Kishner, Andrew, Jr.
Kissinger, Andrew
Kissinger, Mathias
Knox, James

L

Lammey, Andrew
Lapsley, John
Larken, John, Sergt.
Lahsley, John
Laughlin, James
Lawrence, Henry
Learned (Lord), Lieut.
Lee, Sefinah
Lee, Zacarias
Lemaster, Richard
Lemaster, Thomas (Scout)
Lesley, John
Lesley, William
Lesley, William, Sergt.
Lester, John
Lester, Samuel
Lewis, Andrew, Col.
Lewis, Benj., Lieut.
Lewis, Charles, Col.
Lewis, John, Capt. (son of Andrew)
Lewis, John, Capt., (son of Thomas)
Lewis, John, (son of William)
Lewis, Samuel, (brother of General Andrew Lewis)
Lewis, Thomas, (son of General Andrew Lewis)
Lin, Adam
Librough, Henry
Litten, Burton
Litton, Solomon
Litz, William
Lockhart, Jacob
Lockhart, Queavy
Lockridge, Andrew Capt.
Logan, Benj.

Logan, John
Logan, James
Logan, Hugh
Long, Joseph, Ensign
Lord (Leord), Lieut.
Love, Joseph
Love, Phillip, Capt.
Luellen, Thomas
Lucas, Charles
Lucas, Charles, Jr.
Lucas, Henry
Lucas, John
Lucas, William
Luney, Michael
Lybrook (Librough), Henry
Lybrook (Librough), Palser
Lyhnan, Richard
Lyle, John
Lyn, James
Lynch, —
Lyons, Wm.

M

Madison, John
Mann, John
Mann, William
Marks, John
Martin, John
Martin, Brice
Martin, Christian
Martin, George, Sr.
Martin, George, Jr.
Martin, Philip
Martin, Wm., Col.
Matthews, George, Capt.
Matthews, Sampson
Maxwell, Bezaleel
Maxwell, David
Maxwell, John
Maxwell, Thomas
Mayse, Joseph
McAllister, Wm.
McAfee, George
McAfee, James
McAfee, Robert
McAfee, Samuel
McAfee, William
McBride, James
McBride, Joseph
McCallister, James
McCallister, William
McCandless, John
McCastem, Wm.
McCartney, James
McCartney, John
McClanahan, Absalom
McClanahan, Alexander, Capt.
McClanahan, John (Canoe man)
McClanahan, Robert, Capt.
McClintic, Wm.
McClure, John
McClure, Thomas
McCorkle, Wm.
McCrary, (McCreary), Thomas
McCutcheon, Wm.
McCoy, Wm., Lieut.
McCune, William
McDonald, Daniel
McDonald, James
McDowell, Archibald
McDowell, M., Capt.
McDowell, Samuel
McElhaney, Francis
McFarland, Robert
McFarland, William
McGee, John
McGeehey, Samuel
McGinness, John
McGlahlen, John
McGuff, John
McGuff, Patrick
McKee, Wm.
McKinnett, Alex.
McKinney, John
McKinsey, Henley
McKinsey, Moredock
McLaughlin, Edward
McMullen, Wm.
McMullin, John
McNiel, Peter
McNeal, (Niel), John
McNiel, Daniel, Lieut.
McRoberts, Samuel
McNutt, James, Capt.
McNutt, Alexander
Mead, Nicholas
Mead, Thomas
Meader, Israel
Meek, William
Mercer, Hugh
Messersnuth, Barnett
Messersnuth, John
Milican, John
Miller, James
Miller, Robert
Mills, John
Milwood, George
Miner, Henry
Mitchell, James, Capt.
Mitchell James
Mitchell, Thomas
Monadue, Henry
Moffat (Manford), Robert, Capt.
Moffat, George, Capt.
Montgomery, James, Capt.
Montgomery, Samuel
Moody, John
Moon, Abraham
Moore, Andrew, Lieut.
Moore, Frederick
Moore, Hugh
Moore, John
Moore, Moses
Moore, William
Mooney, Frederick
Mooney, Hendly, Ensign
Mooney, Hugh
Mooney, lames
Mooney, John
Mooney, Moses
Mooney, Nicholas
Mooney, Samuel

Mooney, William
Morrow, James
Morrow, James, Jr.
Mullin, Thomas
Mungle (Mondle), Daniel
Mungle (Mondle), Frederick
Murry, John, Capt.
Myers, William

N

Nail, Dennis
Nail. Thomas
Naut, Martin
Naule (Now), Wm., Capt.
Nave, Conrad
Neale, Wm.
Neville, John
Neville, Joseph
Neely, James, (Cadet)
Neely, William
Newland, Abraham
Newland, Isaac
Niel, John
Nelson, John
Newell, James
Newberry, Joseph
Newland, John
Newman, Walter
Nicholas, John
Nickels, Isaac
Noland, John
Northup,—
Nowell, John
Null, Jacob
Null, John O.

O

Odear, James
Oguillen, Barnett
Oguillen, Duncan
Oguillen, Hugh
Oguillen, John
O'Hara, Robert
O'Hara, Charles, Capt.
O'Hara, William
O'Hara, Henry
Olverson, Joseph
Ormsbey, Daniel
Overstreet, Wm.
Owen, Thomas
Owen, Robert
Owens, David
Owler, Henry
Owler, John

P

Pack, George
Pack, Samuel
Packwood, Richard
Pain, Joseph
Parchment, Peter
Parsons, James
Pate, Jeremiah
Patten, John
Pauling, Henry, Capt.
Paulley, James
Paulley, John
Pawlings, Moses
Paxton, Samuel
Peary, Thomas
Pence, Jacob, Ensign
Perce, Thomas
Peragin, Molastin
Persinger, Jacob
Petty, Benjamin
Peyton, John
Peyton, Rowzie
Pharis, Wm.
Pierce, Lieut.
Pierce, John
Plumkenpel, Zacharias
Poague, Wm., Sergt.
Poling, Matthew
Porter, Robert
Posey, Thomas, Commissary
Potter, Thomas
Preston, William
Price, James
Price, Reese
Price, Richard
Price. Thomas
Price, William
Pricket (Pucket), Drury
Priest, David
Pright, John
Prince, William
Prior (Pryor), John

R

Rains, Roberts
Remsey, Josiah
Ranis, Robert
Rapp, Frederick
Ratcliff, Matthew
Ratcliff, William
Ravenscroft, Thomas
Roy, William
Razor, Michael
Reed, Alexander
Read, John, Ensign
Reagh, Archibald
Reagh, John
Reary, James
Reburn (Rayburn), John
Rediford, Benjamin
Reese, Andrew
Reid, Andrew
Reid, Thomas
Reynolds, John
Richardson, Benj.
Richardson, William
Riley, John
Roay, Joseph
Roberts, John
Robinson, Elijah
Robertson, James
Robertson, Thomas, Major
Robertson, Wm., Lieut.
Robinson, Julius
Robinson, William
Robinson, Isaac
Roe, Capt.

Rogers (Rodgers), Andrew
Rogers (Rodgers), Chesley
Rogers (Rodgers), David
Rogers (Rodgers), James
Rogers (Rodgers), Thomas
Rogers (Rodgers), William
Rollens, Richard
Ross, Edward
Ross, Tavener
Rowan, Francis
Rucker, George
Ruddle (Riddle), George
Rue, Abraham
Russell, William, Capt.
Rutherford, Benj.

S

Samples, Samuel
Sanders, James
Sappington, Daniel
Salisbury, William
Savage, John
Savage, Samuel
Sawyers, John
Sayres, John
Seails, William
Sarbara, James
Scard, Lieut.
Scott, Archelous
Scott, Archibald
Scott, Daniel, Capt.
Scott, George
Scott, James
Scott, William
See, Michael
Sedbery, John
Seed, Francis
Selby, James
Sevier, John, Capt.
Sevier, Valentine
Sham, John
Shannon, John
Shannon, Samuel
Sharp, Abraham
Sharp, John (Scout)
Sharp, Edward
Shaw, Henry
Shelby, Evan, Capt.
Shelby, Isaac, Lieut.
Shelby, James
Shelby, William, Capt.
Shell, Arnold
Shelp, John
Shillin, John
Shoat, Emanuel
Simpkins, Daniel
Simpkins, James
Simms, Charles
Simmerman, George
Simpson, James
Simpson, John
Simpson, William
Skaggs, Reuben
Skaggs, Zach.
Skidmore, John, Capt.
Slaughter, George
Slaughter, Francis, Capt.
Slaughter, Lawrence
Smith, Bruten
Smith, Conrad
Smith, David
Smith, Daniel
Smith, Daniel, Jr.
Smith, Edward
Smith, Ericus
Smith, James
Smith, John
Smith, Mecagh
Smith, Moses
Smith, Robert
Smith, William
Smithers, Gabriel
Sobo, George
Spicer, William
Spratt, Isaac, Sergt.
Squires, Uriah
Staffy, Michael
Stailey, Martin
Steele, Andrew
Steele, John
Stephens, John, Lieut.
Stephens, Stephen
Stephens, Thomas
Stephens, William
Stephenson, Hugh, Capt.
Stephenson, Robert
Sterns, Conrad
Stevens, —
Steward, John
Steward, Walter
Stewart, John
Stewart, William
St. Lawrence, Patrick
Stuart, John, Capt.
Stull, Martin
Stump, Michael
Stump, Martin
Sullivan, James
Sullivan, Samuel
Summers, Charles
Swoop, John

T

Tate, T., Lieut.
Tate, William
Tarney, (Farney), Peter
Taylor, Daniel
Taylor, Isaac
Taylor, Seiltor
Taylor, William
Teasy, William
Terrence (Torrence), Andrew
Thomas, Edward
Thompson, Andrew (Ensign)
Thompson, Richard
Thompson, Robert
Thompson, William
Tipton, John
Todd, James
Todd, John
Trent, — (canoe master)
Trent, Obediah
Trimble, Isaac

Trimble, James
Trotter, John
Trotter, Richard
Tucker, William
Tyler, Isaac

V

Vails, John
Vallendingham, George
VanBibber, Isaac
VanBibber, Jesse
VanBibber, Jacob
VanBibber, John
VanBibber, Mathias
VanBibber, Peter
Vance, Edward
Vance, Sampel, Lieut.
Vanhook, Samuel
Vaut (Vaught), Andrew
Vaut (Vaught), Christian
Vaut(Vaught), George
Venable, William
Vaughan (Vaun), John
Vanhook Samuel

W

Waggoner, Andrew
Waggoner, Henry
Waggoner, Henry, Jr.
Walker, Adam
Walker, Henry
Walker, James
Wallace, Andrew
Wallace, Adam Ensign
Wallace, David
Wallace, Robert
Wallace, Samuel, Lieut.
Walter, Michael
Wambler, George
Wambler, Mitchell
Ward, David, Ensign
Ward James, Capt.
Ward. William, Sergt.
Warwick, Jacob
Walter, Michael
Ward, David
Washburn, James
Washburn, Steven
Watkins, Robert
Watson, Jonathan
Waugh, Cadet
Weaver, Christian
Weaver, Michael
Welch, James
Welch, John
Welch, Thomas
Welch, Thomas, Jr.
Wells, Bazaleel
Wells, Samuel
Welsh, Christopher
Wetzel, John
Wetzel, Martin
Whish, Richard
White, David
White, Joseph
White, Solomon
White, William
Whitley, Moses
Whitticor, Joseph
Whitton, Jeremiah
Whitton, Thomas
Whitton, Thomas, Jr.
Wiles, Robert
Wiley, Robert
Wiley, James
Wiley, Robert, Jr.
Wiley, Thomas
Williams, Alden
Williams, David
Williams, Isaac
Williams, James
Williams, Jarrett
Williams, John
Williams, Mack
Williams, Philip
Williams, Richard
Williams, Rowland
Williams, Samuel
Williams, Thomas, Sergt.
Williamson, Aldin
Williamson, David
Willis, Henry
Wilmoth, William
Wilson, Benjamin
Wilson, Edward
Wilson, George
Wilson, James
Wilson, John, Capt.
Wilson, Thomas
Wilson, Wm., Sergt.
Wilson, Samuel
Woods, Adam
Woods, Andrew
Woods, Archibald
Woods, James, Sergt.
Woods, Joseph
Woods, Michael, Capt.
Woods, Richard
Woolsley, Richard
Workman, Daniel
Woodburn, James
Woodburn, Stephen

Y

Young,—

APPENDIX

CONGRESSIONAL DECLARATION

There was raised upon the floor of Congress, April, 1936, the question of the observance of the first battle of the American Revolution. Immediately the question was propounded by Hon. Sol Bloom, a recognized patron of History, "Where was it fought and when was it fought?"

The erection of a monument, the dedicatory speech of Hon. Edward Everett Hale, the inscription of Emerson's Concord Ode upon the Lexington Monument was cited as evidence and there came the further challenge—"You fellows had better learn your history."

We refer Mr. Bloom and the members of both branches of Congress to the accompanying statement, together with the brochure THE BATTLE OF POINT PLEASANT, FIRST BATTLE OF THE AMERICAN REVOLUTION, herein, containing the consensus of leading historians; the enactment of the Congress of the United States; of the State of West Virginia and in lieu of a hymn, to be inscribed, there will be upon the base of the Point Pleasant Battle monument at Point Pleasant (to which the Congress has already contributed, "AS OF THE REVOLUTION"), a Roster of 1,122 names of participants of that battle, fought October 10, 1774, official report of which was never made by General Andrew Lewis. The Roster to be inscribed upon a structural base, yet necessary, which we hope and believe the Congress will gratefully supply. This we hope, to be followed by a National Celebration and Dedication; the Masonic Grand Lodge of the United States to dedicate the base and tablets following the precedent whereby the Masonic Grand Lodge of West Virginia, by special dispensation dedicated the towering eighty-four foot shaft October 9 (the 10th being Sunday), 1909, witnessed by an assemblage of thirty thousand people. There will be room enough and honor enough for all to share in lifting anew the banner of patriotism to which the world will pay homage.

THE BATTLE PRECIPITATED

The Resolution of Lord North was presented to the British House of Parliament of date May, 1774, whereby it was proposed to further supply the American Allied Indians with arms, ammunition and tomahawks. To this procedure, barbaric even beyond Indian conception, the younger Pitt protested, in a speech yet so largely quoted as one of the world's most outstanding orations, when he (Pitt) warned the Parliament that "if the North resolution prevailed it would not only lose the hearts of the American Colonists, but thc Colonies as well."

The first incoming ship to America brought the tidings and further aroused the indignation of the Colonies, who had been speeding by correspondence the convening of the Continental Congress soon to assemble in the City of Philadelphia.

The Colonists, by their original Charter, had been granted territorial rights "from coast to coast." They had protected the Colonies from Indian attacks; they had colonized and established all the forms of Civil Government they might, and had contributed the expense attendant thereto. But they were not privileged to select their own Governors or have representation in the House of Parliament. They were compelled to pay taxes levied by the Crown without voice in the Parliament of England. They had been protesting against such injustice for years.

Following Braddock's defeat, 1755, the Colonists carried the French and Indian Wars to a conclusion within the Colonies, to the great advantage of Great Britain.

While England applauded the Colonies for their most valuable contribution, she at the same time feared their resourcefulness and courage.

Following the Braddock Massacre England hastened to make allies among the Indian Nations. When the Battle of Quebec was fought she had then acquired 100,000 Indian allies. By the aid of thousands of them available she was enabled to drive the French out of Quebec and Canada. 1759, France was then obliged to cede that territory to England, not concluded by treaty until 1763.

In the meantime all of the North West Territory had been ceded by England to the allied Indians of America with the guarantee of being kept as their homes and happy hunting grounds, and guaranteed by England to be protected and kept inviolate from occupation by the Colonists.

The Colonies had been officially notified of the restrictions placed against their going upon what they believed and knew was their own rightful territory, and the resistance to England was fomenting speedily throughout the Colonies.

John Adams, of Massachusetts, fixed the date of "Colonial Decision as of 1764" before the Battle of Point Pleasant was fought and England long knew the war was inevitable.

When the news of the Parliamentary enactment of May 1774 reached the Colonists, carried to them by the first incoming ship from England, the Indians had already been incited to and were making attacks upon the inhabitants below the Ohio River and the frontiersmen were calling for relief.

Virginia, learning of the NORTH RESOLUTION, indignation and resentment thereof was unbounded. She was eager not alone to protect her frontier, but to assert her rights to territory held in common with Massachusetts and Connecticut. She hastened to take up arms to assert her own rights although not herself making a general declaration of war.

It was Virginia that defended it and it was to Virginia the North West Territory was ceded by the Indians, they yielding their bravest warriors as hostages for the maintenance of inviolate peace for three years. Thus enabling Virginia (instead of having to protect her frontier) to go into the Revolution.

The Continental Congress had already been convened a month (September, 1774), when the Battle of Point Pleasant was fought October 10, 1774, the First Battle of the American Revolution.

The order of the Virginia House of Burgesses of which Col. Andrew Lewis was then a member was to assemble an army to march in two separate divisions, one commanded by Governor Dunmore in person, the other by Col. Andrew Lewis, who was in command, to assemble an army, both wings to meet at the mouth of the Kanawha river and from thence to pursue the Indians into their own country, north of the Ohio river, and there subdue them.

This plan, however, as the world now knows, was thwarted as to the place of conflict, when the traitorous Dunmore failed to join Lewis at the mouth of the Kanawha river and they to march together into the "enemy's country."

The treaty between the Indians that ceded to Virginia the North West Territory was in effect until the surrender of Yorktown. Virginia made a gift of that entire Territory to the United States, 1784, ultimately making possible thereby the adoption of the Constitution, 1787, and the establishment of the United States of America.

TITLE THERETO

The territorial acquisitions following upon the heels of all the chain of events focusing, as they did, both before and after the Battle of the American Revolution at Point Pleasant (October 10, 1774) would establish a right of inheritance to land title in any courts of justice of the nation. You will find that the title of Virginia to the North West Territory is legally established by the decision of the Supreme Court of the United States in the case of Handly vs. Anthony, reported in 5 Wheaton 376, in its unanimous opinion being given by Chief Justice Marshall.

Then why should it be questioned as to its having been a Battle of the Revolution as to its right of priority; the honor that the

Congress of the United States has so rightfully recognized (See Senate Bill No. 160, February 17, 1908).

The Bill of Congress was passed without a dissenting voice or discussion.

Following the surrender of Cornwallis at Yorktown, by the treaty at Paris, England ceded to Virginia, not to the Colonists, mark you, all of the North West Territory, that she had previously ceded to the Indians and they to Virginia.

The ceding of the North West Territory by Virginia made possible the organization of the United States Government and the adoption of the Constitution of the United States. It was without money or without price, save the blood of the men of the battle. That acquisition was the result of the Battle of Point Pleasant and makes that Battle the furthest reaching in results of any battle ever fought upon the American Continent.

APPENDIX

Tu-Endie-Wei State Park

Formerly West Virginia Battle Monument State Park

Here at the confluence of the Kanawha and Ohio Rivers, the bloody, day-long Battle of Point Pleasant was fought. On October 10, 1774, Colonel Andrew Lewis' 1,100 Virginia militiamen decisively defeated a like number of Indian forces led by the Shawnee Chieftain Cornstalk.

Long recognized as the decisive engagement in a protracted series of Indian wars now known as Lord Dunmore's War, the Battle of Point Pleasant has become officially known as the "First Battle of the Revolution." This action broke the power of the Indians in the Ohio Valley and quelled a general Indian war on the frontier. Significantly, it also prevented an Indian alliance with the British, one which could very possibly have caused the Revolution to have had a different outcome, as well as having altered the entire history of the U.S. In addition, the ensuing peace with the Indians enabled western Virginians to re-cross the Alleghenies to aid Revolutionary forces.

Fought on this point of land known by the Wyandotte Indian phrase "tu-endie-wei" or "the point between two waters," the battle raged all day. At times Cornstalk and his braves held the upper hand, but eventually the backwoodsmen proved superior on the then, heavily forested battlefield. At the end, over two hundred Indians were killed and more than 50 Virginians had lost their lives, including Colonel Charles Lewis, brother of the commanding officer.

Situated in the southern end of the town of Point Pleasant (#1 Main Street), two-acre Point Pleasant Battle Monument State Park commemorates the engagement. The park's centerpiece is an 84-foot granite obelisk that honors the Virginia militiamen

who gave their lives during the battle, while the statue of a frontiersman stands at the base. Smaller memorial tablets in the park are dedicated to Cornstalk and to "Mad" Anne Bailey whose 'mad' exploits in thwarting the Indians earned her the nickname, after her first husband, Richard Trotter, was killed in the battle. Another interesting marker rests on the spot where Joseph Celoron de Blainville, a French explorer, buried a leaden plate in 1749, claiming the land for his country.

Located on the park is Mansion House. Erected in 1796 by Walter Newman as a tavern, it is the oldest, hewn log house in the Kanawha Valley. Preserved as a museum, it features displays of antiques and heirlooms of the era, including a large square piano believed to be one of the first brought over the Alleghenies. Two bedrooms are furnished with authentic four-poster beds, which are well over 150 years old.

The Colonel Charles Lewis Chapter, N.S.D.A.R. maintains Mansion House Museum and uses it for a chapter house as well.

Point Pleasant Battle Monument State Park is open year-round, and the museum is open from May through October 31.

The Mansion House, situated in Tu-Endie-Wei Park, was built in 1796 by Walter Newman for a tavern. It was the first hewn log house built in the County and was used as an inn, residence, and place of public entertainment. Later additions were made and the building modernized, but it was restored to its original state in 1901 by the first DAR Chapter Regent, Dr. Livia Simpson Poffenbarger aided by the citizens of Point Pleasant and Mason County. In that year the State Legislature appointed the local chapter, DAR to be the custodian of the building, since which time it has been furnished in colonial style, made a repository for historic relics and used as the Colonel Charles Lewis DAR Chapter House.

The Legislature of West Virginia made provisions in 1913 for its permanent maintenance under the supervision of the Point Pleasant Battle Monument Commission; Messrs. J. W. Windon, President; John A. Austin, Secretary; and Charles C. Bowyer, Treasurer.

Tu-Endie-Wei Park is the site upon which was established the headquarters of General Andrew Lewis, from which he commanded the Battle of Point Pleasant, October 10, 1774.

Colonel Charles Lewis, Ann Bailey, Cornstalk and the other heroes of the battle lie buried in this park.

Docents from the local DAR chapter provide visitors with information about the museum, the park and the Battle.

APPENDIX IV

FORT RANDOLPH RESTORATION

THE FORT RANDOLPH COMMITTEE

On August 29, 1996, the Fort Randolph Foundation reorganized to revive the importance of such a historical treasure. New officers and a board of directors were elected to promote the development of fort Randolph as a historic landmark. New period buildings were erected at the fort to display and depict early pioneer life, as it existed in the 1770s.

This 18th century replica is located at Krodel Park in Point Pleasant, Mason County, West Virginia. It was constructed in honor of the American Revolution's Bicentennial celebration and dedicated on October 10, 1974. The original Fort Randolph was built near the confluence of the Great Kanawha and Ohio Rivers in May, 1776—in honor of Peyton Randolph. It was at this fort that the murder of Cornstalk, Shawnee Chief, occurred.

Among the many additions and accomplishments since August, 1996, by the Fort Randolph Foundation to the Fort is the construction of a cabin there within; a 24′ x 42′ trading post built inside the Fort; a 2,250′ walking trail; and, the importation, re-assembling and resurrection of an authentic 1½ story log pioneer cabin directly outside the perimeters of the Fort.

Much progress has been completed within a short period of time. We continue to solicit financial assistance in order to aid our momentum. Point Pleasant's pivotal role in the Revolutionary War is being greatly expanded and recognized by historians and national societies, and we feel these improvements are a vital link in tying our past to the present and future.

HISTORY OF FORT RANDOLPH

The first fort stood on the apex of the upper angle formed by the confluence of the Great Kanawha and Ohio Rivers. It was built in November, 1774, and named Fort Blair, after John Blair, by Captain William Russell who was both the designer and builder. Captain Russell evacuated the fort June, 1775, and it was destroyed.

Captain Mathew Arbuckle was ordered to rebuild the fort in May of 1776 and he named it Fort Randolph in honor of Peyton Randolph. It was in this fort that the murder of Cornstalk, the Shawnee chief, occurred. For some unknown cause, the fort was evacuated in 1779 and was burned by the Indians.

Probably in 1785, another fort was erected for the protection of the inhabitants during the Indian Wars. It was on the Ohio River bank, fifty rods above its predecessors. Colonel Thomas Lewis was in charge.

Fort Randolph was reconstructed in honor of the American Revolution Bicentennial. Groundbreaking was on October 13, 1973, and its dedication was on October 13, 1974.

FORT RANDOLPH — 1996-1999

Built in 1974 for the Battle of Point Pleasant Bicentennial, the Fort has stood on the edge of Krodel Lake for a quarter of a century, used from time to time by civic organizations, clubs and youth programs (4Hers and Boy Scouts). For the most part of those 25 years, the Fort stood empty.

In early spring of 1997, the Fort Committee, with funding from the Claude Worthington Benedium Foundation, Greater Kanawha Resource Conservation & Development Area (RC&D) and the Governor's Community Partnership Grant Program, built a hewed-log structure now used as a trading post and museum. The building is 48′ long and 28′ wide. In addition to the trading post, an 1840 log house was reconstructed adjacent to the Fort in 1997. After acquiring additional funding from RC&D, a beautiful stone fireplace and chimney was added to the log house.

In 1998, the Fort Committee received funding from the Gordon C. and Mildred R. Jackson Foundation and the Governor's Community Partnership Grant Program to build two blockhouses at the front corners of the Fort. Another grant from the Jackson Foundation enabled the committee to construct a 12′ x 24′ hewed-log Blacksmith Shop that was recently completed.

In May of 1998, Fort Randolph opened its gates to the public for viewing and was open every first weekend thru October of that year. This year the Fort has been open every weekend, using a special theme on the first weekend of each month. The Fort has offered our visitors a number of demonstrations and re-enactments. Colonial carpentry, broom making, native Indian lore, candle dipping, basket weaving, soap making, spinning wheel demonstrations, flintlock and cannon demonstrations, flint napping and colonial blacksmithing have been added to the list.

There also is a nature trail built around the Fort and additions are being made by RC&D at this time, including trees and shrubs that are native to this area. A watering system was added this past summer so the plants could be cared for during the dry seasons.

The Fort Randolph Committee has twelve members who have, along with other volunteers, contributed well over 2,000 man-hours of volunteer work since recordkeeping of these hours started. Construction and other improvement costs, over the past three years, have exceeded $3,000.

Since opening day, May 1, 1999, the Fort has greeted over 3,000 visitors to date. There has been one wedding and 4H Club and Boy Scout camp-outs. During Battle Days there are encampment and battle re-enactments along with demonstrations and story telling.

SOURCES OF FUNDING

- Claude Worthington Benedum Foundation
- Greater Kanawha Resource Conservation Development
- West Virginia Division of Culture and History
- Governor's Community Partnership Program
- WV State Legislature Funding For Parks
- The Gordon C. and Mildred R. Jackson Foundation
- The City of Point Pleasant
- Monetary donations by fort visitors
- Items for display in the museum have been donated by many individuals and are greatly appreciated.

FACTS ABOUT FORT RANDOLPH, POINT PLEASANT, WV

This fort was built during 1973-74 and dedicated on October 10, 1974. The fort's approximate size is 65 yards wide and 60 yards deep. Two 34′ x 22′ log cabins are located at the rear corners of the fort.

In 1997, a 48′ x 28′ trading post was built between the aforementioned log cabins.

In 1997, a 20′ x 18′ 1½ story hewed-log house, circa 1840, was reconstructed outside the Fort.

In 1998, two blockhouses were constructed at the front corners of the fort. The lower levels measure 12′ x 12′ and the upper levels measure 16′ x 16′.

In 1999, a hewed log blacksmith shop measuring 12′ x 24′ was constructed.

Construction and maintenance continues by the Fort Randolph Foundation volunteers as funds become available.

Anyone wishing to assist in the restoration and maintenance of this significant Revolutionary War Memorial may contact the:

Fort Randolph Committee
Point Pleasant, WV 25550

APPENDIX V

Battle Days Celebration

The residents of the town first commemorated the Battle of Point Pleasant in the 1800s. Dr. Livia Simpson Poffenbarger began in the 1890s to hold a public memorial service to honor the men who had fought and died at the Battle. Dr. Poffenbarger pushed for the organization of a local chapter of the National Society Daughters of the American Revolution.

She also began the drive to erect a suitable monument at the site of the Battle. Her efforts were unsuccessful at first. The site of the Battle itself fell into a state of great disrepair. In 1901 Dr. Poffenbarger renewed her drive to properly commemorate the Battle of Point Pleasant. This time she was successful in obtaining funding from Congress to erect a monument at the Point. Congress further declared the Battle of Point Pleasant to be "a battle of the American Revolution."

Also in 1901, the Colonel Charles Lewis Chapter of the National Society Daughters of the American Revolution was formed. This chapter recently celebrated its 100th anniversary with a luncheon honoring past members and descendants. Dr. Poffenbarger was its first Chapter Regent.

The work of establishing a proper memorial began upon receiving Congressional funding. The area known as the Point was cleared and work began on erecting an obelisk in the park. Livia Poffenbarger single-handedly saved "The Mansion House." It had literally been shoved over the hill toward the Ohio River in an effort to clear the parkland. She ordered it brought back up the bank and restored for use as a museum.

The monument was dedicated on October 10, 1909. A huge celebration was held at the Point, during which an estimated 10,000 people attended.

However, after Livia's death, public interest in the annual memorial service waned. The Daughters of the American Revolution continued with the annual service but attendance was sparse.

During the 1960s and early 1970s the Memorial Service continued. The only attendees were usually D.A.R. members and a few historically-minded citizens of the county. The Main Street merchants held annual "Battle Days" sidewalk sales in an effort to renew interest in the celebration of the Battle.

As the 200th anniversary of the Battle approached in 1974, the community became interested in commemorating the Battle in a big way. A replica of Fort Randolph had been erected near Krodel Park Lake in the city park. As part of the 1974 celebration, a pageant was performed at the Fort. There was also a battle re-enactment at Krodel Park and numerous other festive activities. There was also a solemn Memorial Service for the men who fought and died at the Battle.

The 200th anniversary celebration brought renewed attention to the Battle of Point Pleasant. This interest continued unabated through America's Bicentennial Celebration in 1976.

In the 1980s, as interest in the Battle once again seemed to wane, Main Street Point Pleasant was formed. Under the Main Street USA banner, this organization aims to revitalize and improve the downtown area of Point Pleasant.

In 1992 the Battle of Point Pleasant Memorial Committee was formed under the Main Street Point Pleasant umbrella. The aim of the Committee was to promote, commemorate and celebrate the Battle of Point Pleasant on October 10, 1774.

During the first few years the annual event was held on the weekend nearest October 10th each year. Later, as the annual celebration became a nationwide event, the Committee designated the first full weekend in October as the date for what had become known as "Battle Days."

The first few years of the renewed efforts saw an encampment consisting of only two men. One year the Brigade of the American Revolution encamped at the Point during Battle Days.

A local chapter of the National Society, Sons of the American Revolution was formed in 1994. As this Chapter became more and more active in Battle Days, they assumed responsibility for the Memorial Service held on Sunday of each year's commemoration. The Memorial Service has become a national event featuring S.A.R. Chapters from seven states and the National Society.

The encampment has grown to include many tents and demonstrations. Sutlers, merchants and a tavern also occupy the Park during Battle Days.

The Committee was honored to have the President's Own, "The Old Guard," participate in Battle Days for three years. The Old Guard led the parade each year and presented a concert in their own inimitable style on the Point. In addition, The Old Guard honored the dead by providing an Honor Guard and music at the Memorial Service on Sunday.

Local merchants have been generous benefactors for the Battle Days Committee from its inception. Each year a number of businesses purchase a steer at the Mason County Fair; this steer is then donated to the Committee for their annual ox roast. The ox is prepared in the traditional way—by slow roasting overnight in a pit—before being served the following day with beans slow-cooked over an open fire.

Another annual event hosted by the Committee is the Colonial Ball. With music provided by the Anonymous String Band, the Ball is eagerly anticipated and attended by visitors from all over the United States. While Colonial attire is not required, many attendees dress for the period, making this a colorful and enjoyable dance.

A relatively new event that has quickly become a crowd favorite is the lantern tour of Tu-Endie-Wei Park. Costumed interpreters present first-person narratives regarding the persons and events which comprise Point Pleasant's historic past.

The highlight of the annual Battle Days celebration for many, however, is the Living History Day for area students presented on Friday of each year's event. Stations are established throughout the Park demonstrating different aspects of Colonial life. Students are taught skills used during the Colonial period, especially in the Virginia frontier, which included Point Pleasant. The students also learn songs and games as well as attending a Colonial magic show. Although geared toward fourth grade students, last year's Living History Day was also attended by over two hundred middle school students.

Battle Days continues to expand and improve each year. In 2000 a chili cook-off was added to Saturday's activities. Dubbed "Burning Down the Bridge" for its location under the Bartow Jones Bridge, the cook-off was sponsored by the Point Pleasant Farmers' Market. The year 2000 also marked the first successful year for the "Miss Battle Days" pageant. Girls ages 5-7, 7-12 and 16-18 competed for titles and prizes. The teenagers also competed for the right to be a contestant for the State "Fairs and Festivals" title the following year.

As the years pass, it is hoped that Battle Days will continue to improve upon its success. Through the efforts of the Battle of Point Pleasant Memorial Committee, the Battle of Point Pleasant will be commemorated for many generations to come.

INDEX